What's on
in and around
Oxford

by

Angela Hewitt

Travelling
Gourmet
Publications

Travelling Gourmet Publications:

Cooking on the Move
A cookery book for caravanners, campavanners and boaters cooking in a confined mobile kitchen. Price: 4.50

What's Cooking in the New Forest. Second edition. Price 4.95

What's Cooking on the Isle of Wight. Second edition. Price 4.75

What's Cooking in the Cotswolds. Price 4.95

What's Cooking in and Around Brighton. Price 4.95

What's Cooking in and Around Oxford. Price 4.95

The Herb Growers Recipe Book and Directory of Herb Specialists. Price 3.45

Taste of Herbs
- Lavender - Mint - Elderflowers - Parsley - Tarragon - Basil -
A gift pack containing a sachet of herbs complete with 7 delicious recipes. Price 2.25 each.   Mixed Pack of 6. Price 6.95.

Published by: Travelling Gourmet Publications
Padmore Lodge, Beatrice Avenue
East Cowes, Isle of Wight

Written, designed and illustrated by: Angela Hewitt
Copy Right: What's Cooking Series: Travelling Gourmet Publications
Printed and bound in England by: Itchen Printers ltd.

Recommended Price £4.95

What's Cooking
in and around
Oxford

*Recipes from many Restaurants, Cafes,
Tearooms, Pubs, Producers and Suppliers
in Oxford and its surrounding area*

*The definitive guide to cooking,
shopping and eating out.*

*This book is dedicated
to all those who believe small is beautiful, and to all those
individual food and catering businesses who dedicate their
lives to personally providing only the best in food and
service.*

*And to all of you; tourists and locals alike, who support
these businesses and by doing so keep our unique heritage
alive.*

Contents

Introduction	7
Oxford City	9
Out of Town	10
Starters	11
Light Lunches and Vegetarian Dishes	27
Fish and Shellfish	43
Meat, Poultry and Game	50
Puddings and Desserts	69
Afternoon Teas	80

Food Files:
The Shopping Basket	13
The Great British Pub	20
Salads Herbs from Halcyon	25
Vegetarian Cookery	30
The Herb Garden	32
Oxford Waterways	47
The Value of Meat	53
The Hygienic Kitchen	56
Cask of a Thousand Years	63
The Covered Market	67
Simple Classic Salad Sauces	68
Self Pick Farms	72
Let's Bake a Cake	82

Town and Village Guide	89
Index of Contributors	91
Measurements and Conversions	93
Index of Recipes	94

Cooking Notes

Oven Temperatures Vary particularly in fan ovens which can be hotter and should be reduced a notch. Old ovens can also vary. The temperatures in this book are only a guide to what the optimum oven should be.

Measurements should not be mixed. Stick to one or the other, imperial or metric.

Baking Blind means to line an uncooked pastry case with greaseproof paper or tin foil then fill with dried beans. This acts as a weight and prevents the pastry from rising in the centre and collapsing around the side during baking. The case should be cooked in a hot oven for 15-20 minutes or until the pastry is cooked and a pale golden colour.

Pastry is sometimes called for in a recipe without giving precise instructions. if 8oz-225gm of pastry is required, this means pastry made with 8oz-225gm of plain flour. If using ready made pastry then 12oz-350gm is usually required.

Bain Marie or Water Bath, is a large roasting pan or saucepan filled with hot water in which a smaller dish or basin containing the food is placed. The idea is to keep a difficult sauce i.e bernaise, warm, or to protect the sides of something delicate while it is being cooked in the oven, for instance a baked egg custard.

Introduction

Just one day in Oxford and I was scuttling home with an armful of produce, eager to cook some good traditional English sustenance. Nothing fancy, just robust ingredients, of which there is a good deal in Oxford, simply treated so as not to obscure the wholesome, natural flavours.

The variety of ingredients available to the shopper is just a snippet of what is going on in Oxford. Cooking is excellent and inspirational, from the freshly baked breads and cakes at bread shops and patisseries to the wealth of cooking that is going on in the many reputable cafes and restaurants. Despite influences from abroad, particularly France, many of the dishes reflect a leaning towards robust English tastes.

Food is rich and often luxurious and one gets the sense that the Oxford community from the student to the don is a well fed lot, or should be with the choice of eateries and suppliers on offer. Oxfordians, I have no doubt take their eating seriously as would be fitting to such a scholarly place.

Tourists and locals alike might be spoilt for choice, but they will never go hungry or indeed thirsty, a will surely develop a taste for the local cask brewed real ale as well as the wonderful food, from a pub lunch to a restaurant special, that is always on offer.

Happy Eating!

Note to Eaters

The recipes in this book are an example of the kind of cuisine served at each establishment.
Most chefs cook by instinct and use what is seasonally available; therefore, the recipes found in this book are not always featured on their menus.
However, there is always something equally as delicious to be found in its place.

Restaurant Law. When you make a reservation, even by phone, you are entering a legal contract. If for some reason you are unable to keep that reservation please let them know. No matter how short the notice. At least you are giving them a chance to resell the table to a casual caller. Failure to do so could incur a cancellation fee. So, don't spoil your holiday, please let them know.

Oxford City

Originally, in the first few centuries Oxford was known as Oxnaforde - the ford of the oxen. It later became shortened to Oxford and in the fourteenth century it was given an official coat of arms - an ox crossing a ford.

For centuries Oxford went through an up and down history of serious decline and varying revivals. Oxford's most permanent recovery started in the 11th century when a market was established and an annual fair which served to increase revenues for the town. As the university grew it became the strong hold of the city and for the ensuing time, right up until 1890 the university controlled much of what went on in the city.

In 1893 a young William Morris started to make his mark and soon turned a pedal bicycle making industry into a major car manufacturing industry. His industry brought big and fortuitous changes to the economy of Oxford. Today the pedal bicycle is a major form of transport through out the city. Very few cars pass through the streets. The lack of traffic certainly provides a relaxed atmosphere to the town and pedestrians can enjoy a stroll through Oxford at leisure and without having to negotiate their way through treacherous traffic.

The beginnings of Oxford as a scholarly place are dubiously recorded from 1,000 BC. Nevertheless it slowly became known as 'the' place of learning and development. Oxford really came into its own when Henry II fell out with the King of France in 1167. English scholars all of Holy orders who went to France to learn were ordered home, and it is to Oxford that they returned and so began the oldest university in the English speaking world. It also became one of the great architectural centres of the world. Examples of almost every style of building over the last 1,000 years can be found in the city.

It can be said today that Oxford has three strings to its economical bow.

The first, the car industry has not so much declined as reformed over the past 20 years but it is nevertheless still there and providing a good deal of local employment and revenues for local businesses.

Secondly there is the university which of course increases the spending population considerably during term time. But when they go home for their end of term break in move the tourists. They come from all corners of the world to see the architecture, to study the scholarly history and to have fun on the network of waterways that weave their way in and around the city.

There are summer excursions by public cruiser. For the hands on tourist there are punts, canoes, rowing boats and private cruisers to be hired, with plenty of opportunity to stop of for a pint of real ale and a delicious snack at on of the riverside pubs. Alternatively there are plenty of interesting riverside walks for those preferring to stretch their legs, and all of this is accessible from a short stroll out of town.

Out of Town

It's hard to believe if you look around the county now, but not so long ago, in fact little more than 170 years, Oxfordshire was two thirds woodland. The royal forest of Wychwood created by Norman Kings remained unchanged right up until the beginning of the reign of James I. It was indeed a fortuitous area of hills and woods that offered good hunting ground for all kinds of game to keep the Kings hounds and hawks in work; and the web of streams and rivers channelled plenty of watering ground and wide valleys with level ground for the growing of grain. The riches of the land certainly helped to bring about the Oxford we know and love today.

There are several ways to get out of town, by car, bicycle or possibly bus, but the most pleasurable way must be by boat along the river Thames or the river Cherwell. The Cherwell Valley enjoys rambling country side, water meadows, ancient hedgerows and plenty of picturesque villages.

Banbury is a good place to begin a leisurely drive. Travel along the narrow roads that meander between Oxford and Banbury and discover mediaeval churches, quaint thatched stone cottages, and areas of great interest for the naturalist.

The Oxford canal tow-path is a beautiful walk especially if combined with other footpaths, and for cyclists there is more than 60 miles of cycle-ways.

Oxford is a good centre for visiting other major tourist areas such as the Cotswolds and Stratford-upon-Avon. Blenheim Palace, home of the Duke of Marlborough, at Woodstock, is only eight miles away. Any one interested in technology - most young children these days, of both gender- then a visit to the Oxford Science Park is essential. For anyone who desires a holiday filled with interest and a bit of gentle activity rather than a laze on the beach then Oxfordshire is the place to visit.

Starters

As a prelude to a larger meal a starter should be small, light and appetizing. Something to whet the appetite and stimulate the gastric juices.

Many of the starters in this section can be served as a light snack or lunch by increasing the proportions and accompanying with a crisp, lightly dressed salad and freshly baked bread.

When choosing your starter, most important of all is a question of balance. For instance, avoid serving two cream based dishes together, and if you are serving two fish dishes try and make one of them shell fish.

For ease, soup is by far the best option. It can be prepared in advance then re-heated at the last minute. If soup is to be hot make sure it is piping and if cold it should be icy cold.

Whatever your choice, remember a starter is not to be made a meal of, and the emphasis should be on "little and light".

Hot Aubergine and Basil Mousse with Pesto and Spinach

One of head chef Ian Morgan's favourite starters.

3 aubergines
1 clove of garlic
2 shallots
4 basil leaves
pinch of nutmeg
1 fl oz pesto sauce
3oz-75gm creamed cooked spinach
3/4pt fresh tomato concasse
3 tbls picked herbs
3 eggs
¼pt double cream

1...Peel the aubergine, garlic and shallots. Dice and put in a saucepan with the basil. Cook over a gentle heat in a drop of olive oil. When soft puree the vegetables in a blender.
2...Add the eggs and cream and pass through a sieve. Season with salt, pepper and nutmeg.
3...Generously butter 6 ramekins. Divide the aubergine mixture between them and then put in a roasting pan half filled with water. Bake in a pre-heated oven 190c/375f/gas5 for 40-45 minutes.
4...Meanwhile heat the tomato concasse with the pesto sauce and freshly chopped herbs.
5...When the mousses are set (the centres will feel firm to the touch), run a knife around the edge and turn out onto hot plates. Pour the sauce around and garnish with little mounds of
cooked, creamed spinach.

From the kitchen of...

THE BEAR HOTEL
Park Street, Woodstock, Oxford.   Tel: 811511 Fax: 813380
Proprietors: Forte
Chef: Ian Morgan and team.   AA Rosettes
Open all year for lunch and dinner.
Booking advised but casual callers welcome if there's room. Credit cards accepted. Wheelchair access.
Log fire in Winter. Full a la carte menu. Extensive English and Mediterranean menu. Seafood, game and vegetarian dishes.

The Shopping Basket

It is a sad fact that if we don't support our local shops and small producers they will disappear without trace.

The convenience of the supermarket has beguiled us all and yet their fresh produce such as meat, vegetables and bread, food we would normally have bought from the butcher, the baker and the green grocer, is more expensive to buy at the supermarket.

It's true that the supermarket has the edge where staple groceries are concerned, but that is where it begins and ends. An important area where the supermarket falls down is in its disinterest in promoting local produce; for example speciality ice creams, chocolates, biscuits, cheeses, chutneys etc.

When you are on holiday with more time on your hands, and a slower pace to your schedule, you should find the time to search out these small shops and enjoy the traditional pleasures of being served all that delicious local food. There's no shadow of a doubt it has been prepared with loving care, not for the masses but for you, the individual.

Oxford offers shopping for the international gourmet with a taste for robust food. One of the best places to shop is the Covered Market. Traditional butchers offer well hung meat an game, hanging there for everyone to see. There is plenty of game for every season from the common pheasant and mallard to the not so common, woodcock, grouse an hare. Beef is beautifully marbled, lamb is pink and succulent, poultry is free range and full of flavour. Fish mongers provide the community with a wide range of fresh fish but as would be expected of a true fish monger, nothing on Mondays.

Palm's delicatessen has shelves packed with fascinating groceries from around the world. Fasta Pasta a small cosy shop brimming with foods of the sun sells a fabulous range of olives and extra virgin olive oil. Pasta, salads and sauces come fresh as does the ciabatta bread which according to Henrietta Green is the best in the country. The bread is actually made by De Gustibus in the centre of Thame.

Sausages have enjoyed a revival since the late eighties and Stroff's Sausages sell and excellent range. They are packed into natural skins and contain real meat as opposed to the slurry which is packed into the artificial skins of the mass produced sausage. Stroff's has also created a good range of vegetarian sausages.

The Oxford Cheese Company, is figuratively speaking, the cornerstone of the covered market. It offers a large and tempting range of cheeses from around Britain and Europe. All in excellent condition. Look out for Oxford Blue.

Travel out of Oxford and you will find plenty more honest to goodness produce. Farm shops offer their own as well as other peoples produce. Wells store at Abingdon sells over 70 British Cheeses. For your Christmas goose or turkey go to Peach Croft Farm Shop and during the pop along to pick a punnet of ripe juicy strawberries.

Bread is big in and around Oxford. Small bakeries use traditional recipes reminding us of how good bread used to be before white sliced and supermarket destruction. So there is no excuse for offering supermarket pulp to you dinner party guests. And it must be said that gourmets and supporters of British traditions don't need a dinner party for the excuse to break good bread.

To keep this bounty of produce alive it is essential that we support our small local shops and producers. The small shopkeeper is part of our National Heritage. Apart from that we desperately need them and the competition they give the big boys. If they are forced to close through lack of business it is inevitable that supermarkets will have a monopoly and general food prices will climb sky high.

Asparagus Soup

You can PYO asparagus at Peach Croft Farm near Abingdon

½lb-225gm old potatoes
2pts-1.1lt good chicken stock
1lb-450gm asparagus
salt and black pepper
2 or 3 tbls whipping cream, according to taste

1...Peel the potatoes and cut in half. Cook the potatoes in the chicken stock, (use a stainless steel or enamel lined saucepan), until the potatoes fall. Remove from the heat.
2...Trim the tips from the asparagus and put to one side. Cut the hard woody ends off the asparagus then cut them into 1"-2.5cm lengths. Add the potatoes, cover and cook slowly until the asparagus becomes very soft.
3...Put in a blender and whizz until smooth.
4...If you are a perfectionist push the soup through a sieve or for ease a vegetable mouli.
5...Return to a gentle heat and add the whipping cream. The more cream you add the more delicate the flavour. Season well. Serve with crispy croutons.

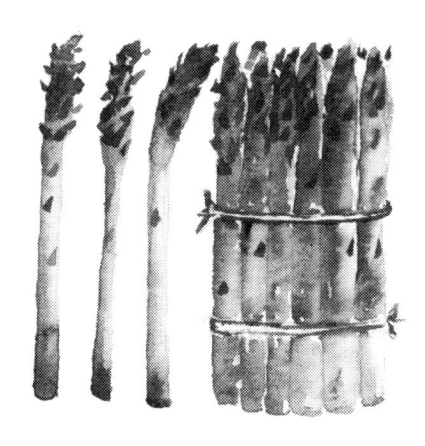

Avocado Cardinale

A traditional Italian starter.

½ avocado per person
2oz-50gm smoked salmon per person
2oz-50gm Atlantic prawns per person
1 hpd tbls 'Marie Rose'/'Salsa Aurora sauce (see pg 68)
thin slices of cucumber and thin slices of tomato
garnish - radichio leaves, lollo rosse, ¼ wedge of lemon and parsley

1...Remove the avocado from its skin, either peel off or scoop out with a large tablespoon. Cut into thin slices and fan out onto good sized plates.
3...Arrange the smoked salmon on the top.
4...Place a cup shaped lettuce leaf on the side and fill with the prawns. Spoon the sauce on top of the prawns. Decorate with the radichio, lollo rosse, lemon wedges and parsley.

From the menu of...

LA GALLERIA
Ristorante Italiano
2 Market Place, Woodstock, Oxon OX20 1TA   Tel/Fax: 01993 813381
Proprietor:Gian Lucio Montanino
Chefs: Paolo Solera and Gian Lucio Montanino
Open: All year. Lunch 12noon-2pm. Dinner 7pm-10pm
Booking advised but casual callers welcome if there's room. Children welcome. Credit cards accepted. Situated in an 18th century building in the centre of Woodstock. Outside seating in the Summer. Serves, game and vegetarian dishes. Specialises in fresh pasta and seafood.

Tjatjiki

A refreshing dip that makes a light starter.

2 pots of Total Greek strained yogurt
4 cloves of garlic, more or less depending on taste
½ peeled cucumber
1 or 2 grated carrots
fresh mint

1...Grate the cucumber and put in a colander until as much juice as possible has strained away and no more liquid is dripping. (Give it a squeeze to make sure).
2...Skin and grate the garlic and mix into the yogurt. Add the grated carrot, the cucumber and as much freshly chopped mint as you want.
3...Serve with vegetable crudits and fingers of toasted pitta bread.

Recipe provided by...

BUNTERS DELICATESSEN
and Post Office
4-6 Hayfield Rd, Oxford OX26TT.
Proprietors: Mr N Vernicos, Mr E Vernicos and Mrs L Vernicos
Chef: Mr N Vernicos
Open: All year. Monday-Saturday 9am-6.30pm and Sunday 10am-2pm
Greek and Italian specialist food shop. Produce their own homemade moussaka, stuffed aubergines, spinach pie, stuffed vine leaves and much more.

Pan Fried Scallop Mousse with Shallot and Chilli Dressing

A fashionable starter for a formal dinner party

8oz-225gm scallop meat
1 whole egg
½pt-275ml double cream
½tspn salt
½tspn cayenne pepper

1...In a blender puree the scallop meat with the whole egg.
2...Place the scallop puree in a bowl and sprinkle with the salt and cayenne pepper. Beat the mixture until it begins to thicken and strengthen.
3...Slowly beat in the double cream until smooth.
4...Divide the mixture into 4 buttered ramekins. Sit them in a roasting tin half filled with water and bake in the oven pre-heated to 200c/400f/gas6 for 25-35 minutes.
5...Allow to cool and remove from the ramekins.
6...Pan fry the mousse' in a little olive oil until golden brown and serve immediately with the shallot and chilli dressing.

Dressing

1 red chilli, finely chopped
1 green chilli, finely chopped
1 shallot, finely chopped
2 tbls of raspberry vinegar
6 tbls of olive oil
salt and pepper

1...Whisk all the ingredients together and check the seasoning.

From the menu of...

FEATHERS HOTEL
Restaurant and Bar
Market Street, Woodstock, OX2 1SX.   Tel: 01993 812291 Fax: 813158
Chef: David Lewis
Open: All year. 7.30am - 9.30pm
Casual callers welcome. Credit Cards accepted.
Outside seating in Summer and Log fire in Winter.
Seafood, game and vegetarian dishes

Chicken Liver Pate

8oz-225gm chicken livers
1 small onion, finely shopped
garlic to taste
1 glass of red wine or a measure of brandy
4oz-110gm soft butter
salt and pepper
sprigs of fresh thyme, leaves stripped
cranberry sauce to serve

1...Melt 1oz-25gm of the butter and gently cook the onion and garlic with the thyme until transparent.
2...Add the chicken livers and cook for 5 minutes. Put in the blender with the soft butter and whiz until a smooth or coarse consistency depending on personal preference.
3...Turn into a terrine or similar container and refrigerate until set.
4...Serve with warm cranberry sauce and toast.

From the kitchen of...

THE COTTAGE BAKERY
and Coffee Shop
44 Bath Street, Abingdon OX14 3QH   Tel: 01235 520972
Proprietor: Paul McKeogh
Open: Winter 8.30am-5pm and Summer 8.30am-5.30pm
Casual callers and children welcome. Wheelchair access.
Vegetarian dishes, morning coffee, light lunches, snacks and afternoon tea. Fresh bread and cakes daily.

The Great British Pub

The British pub is still great, but oh... so very different! Gone is the male dominated enclave where a woman needed permission to enter the bar, where smoked filled rooms were packed with men drowning their sorrows and soothing their private emotions, where the talk was of sport and cars.

Today there are as many women and children in a pub as men; with family rooms that are bigger than the public bar. But most striking of all there is cleanliness. Clean counters, sparkling windows, well hoovered and new carpets, interior design and performance lighting. The now nostalgic smell of ale and cigarettes has all but vanished and a new, fresh, welcoming atmosphere pervades the air.

Where once you were lucky if you could get a cheese and pickle sandwich, now you can get, pizza margharitta, thai style curry, spinach canneloni with Italian tomato sauce, spare ribs, seafood platters, deep-fried potato skins, death by chocolate and creme brulée; for the family Christmas day lunch, Mothering Sunday lunch, Easter Sunday lunch and Father's day lunch.

Many pub goers with faithful memories of the past will say a pub is no longer a pub, but they can't argue that the original concept is still there. A bar still exists for adults only. You can still go in for just a drink. And the drink has greatly improved, both in choice and quality. This is more noticeable in the south of England where crisp lager tends to be more popular than ale and where ale often had the clinical sharpness of mass produced keg beer.

Thanks to CAMRA 'Campaign for Real Ale', real ale brewed in traditional casks by small individual and specialist breweries has finally made its mark. Go into a pub today and you will be confronted with a choice of nutty, rounded, flavoured ales which are extremely palatable, even to a woman's taste buds. Names like Old Speckled Hen, Tangle Foot, Fuggles, Flowers and Directors and some house named brews are becoming a familiar sight.

The choice of drink hasn't just grown in the variety of ales either. Cider is no longer alcoholic pop but is made with good traditional flavour. Wine is no longer just Corrida red or white but a carefully selected, albeit small range, from around the world and many pubs offer English wines such as Damson, Strawberry, Elderberry and Parsnip.

Most pubs are brewery owned and in the seventies they tried very hard to drag them out of the 40's and 50's. They made attempts to enlarge their clientele by making pubs acceptable to women who they knew would drink in a hotel bar with out feeling uncomfortable. They ripped out floors and doors, pulled down walls and put in light and airy hotel style bars and within months saw their profit margins dwindle as the 'real drinkers' moved to pubs that had escaped the hands of brewery developers.

Breweries were quick to recognise their mistake, ripped out the walls and doors and floors once more, and turned them back, as authentically and hygienically as they could into the dream of what a British pub should be. Second time round they succeeded in creating a middle-road of false tradition complete with tatty edges and yokel artefacts, but with spotlessly clean centres, where every walk of life could happily travel.

So, much has changed in the great British pub, but our heritage is still intact. No where in the world is there anything that can compare. The days of 'spit and sawdust' are long gone, but if anything, the great British pub is today, greater for it.

Chicken and Basil Sausage

Serve on a bed of salad leaves with a julienne of beetroot and balsamic vinegar.

Sausage
1lb-450gm skinless chicken, minced
2fl oz double cream
small bunch fresh basil
1oz-25gm red currant jelly
1 egg
½oz-10gm butter
good pinch grated nutmeg
salt and pepper
sausage skins

Dressing
3 tbls olive oil
1 tbls balsamic vinegar
1 tspn honey
1 tspn grain mustard
salt and pepper
mixed salad leaves
1 beetroot

1...Chop the basil leaves and sweat off in the butter then add to the minced chicken along with the salt and pepper, nutmeg and red currant jelly. Beat the egg with the cream and mix into the chicken mixture.
2...Pie the mixture into sausage skins and leave to rest in the fridge for 12 hours.
3...Gently pan-fry the sausages lightly colouring on all sides then finish in a moderate oven for 5 minutes. Allow to cool.
4...Wash the beetroot. Season and wrap in foil. Cook for 3 hours in a moderate oven. Allow to cool then peel and cut into strips.
5...Wash the salad leaves and arrange on 6 plates.

6...Beat together the olive oil, balsamic vinegar, mustard, honey and seasoning to make the dressing.

7...Place the julienne of beetroot on the salad leaves, slice the sausage and arrange on the salad and dribble over the dressing. Sprinkle with freshly chopped basil.

From the kitchen of...

CHERWELL BOATHOUSE
Bardwell Road, Oxford, OX2 6SR.   Tel: 01865 52746   Fax: 01865 399459 (office 391549)
Proprietors: Verdin Family Partnership.
Chef: Gerard Crowley
Open: All year. Lunch, Tuesday - Sunday 12noon-2pm. Dinner, Tuesday - Saturday 6pm-10.30pm.
Closed Dec 24th-30th.
Credit cards accepted.
Outside seating with traditional English river views, with a buzz of activity during the punting season. Specialising in regularly changing menus and seasonal food with a modern flair. Vegetarian dishes

Wiltshire Ham and Green Peppercorn Terrine

Serve with hot crusty roll and butter.

2lb-900gm cooked and diced ham
2 chicken legs, boned and skinned
8oz-225gm streaky bacon
2 tbls green peppercorns, roughly chopped
2 eggs
4oz-110gm button mushrooms, quartered
4 cloves garlic
4oz-110gm cooked and chopped spinach
oil

1...Line a terrine mould with streaky bacon which has been slightly flattened with a rolling pin.
2...Fry the garlic, mushrooms, spinach, ham and peppercorns then allow to cool. Check the seasoning.
2...Blend the chicken legs in a processor. Add the cream. Blend briefly, then pass through a sieve (if, like the Inn for All Seasons you are a perfectionist).
3...When all the ingredients are cold fill the terrine. Start with a layer of ham mixture, then chicken mousse and so on until all used up.
4...Cover the terrine. Place in a bain marie and cook in a pre-heated oven 230c/425f/gas7 for about 45 minutes. Test with a skewer inserted in the middle for 'donness'.
Serve with hot toast and a home made chutney. Serves 12-14 people.

From the menu of...

THE INN FOR ALL SEASONS
The Barringtons, Burford, OX18 4TN.   Tel: 01451 844324 Fax: 01451 844375
Proprietor: Mr Sharp
Open: All year. 8am-2.30pm and 6pm-11pm
Casual callers welcome but booking advised in the restaurant. Credit cards accepted. Wheelchair access. Ample parking. Hotel/Inn/Restaurant.
Log fire in Winter and outside seating in the garden in Summer.
Game and vegetarian dishes. Fish a speciality.

Salad Herbs from Halcyon

It has taken several years getting through, but at last a normal every day salad consists of more than just a few ordinary limp salad leaves. Radichio, frisse, rocket, oak leaf and lambs lettuce, once upon a time called 'designer lettuce' are now being regularly tossed in bowls and coated in glistening dressings all over England.

We have two people to thank for such pleasure. Firstly those enthusiastic restaurant chefs who force fed their diners with a pleasant determination that just had to be swallowed, and secondly the gardeners and crop producers who recognised that this wasn't just another trend, and who for once asked the customer (the restauranteur) what they wanted then went away and grew it. What was once called in the trade 'exotics' soon became communal garden stuff!

I have to confess that even I haven't come across some of the crops on the list at Halcyon herbs at Little Milton. Things like, gold orach, kingston mustard, red mustard, texel greens and zwoische krul.

Richard Bartlett, owner of Halcyon Herbs, followed in his parents footsteps and has been involved in horticulture all his life. He helped to set up the kitchen gardens at Le Manoir aux Quat Saisons. It was there that he developed an interest in growing the unusual crops demanded by such a place as Le Manoir.

When he left Le Manoir aux Quat Saisons to set up his own market garden he had no doubt in which direction he was going. When he is not producing a wide and fascinating range of salads and herbs for some 50 restaurants locally and in London he is searching for new crops to expand his range. This could well turn into a case where the gardener introduces the chef to a few new products.

Gee's Restaurant, one of Richard's customers has supplied two recipes using salad leaves from Halcyon herbs.

You can visit the nursery at: Little Milton
or telephone: 01865 89180 or 0374 723103

Carpaccio of Beef with Mixed Hot Leaves

The herbs and leaves for this recipe can be obtained from Halcyon Herbs

2lb-900gm sirloin of beef
mixed hot leaves eg. American cress, Greek cress, red mustard and wild rocket, about 1oz-25gm per person
2oz-50gm fresh parmesan per person
cracked black peppercorns, done in a pestle and mortar
½ bunch chives, snipped
Dressing:
4 anchovy fillets
1 plump clove garlic
8fl oz extra virgin olive oil
1oz-25gm grated parmesan
1 tbls balsamic vinegar
pinch pepper

1...Remove all fat from the sirloin of beef. Season well and then blacken it over a gas flame or in a hot pan. Dip in iced water to stop it cooking and then refrigerate for 2 hours.
2...Place all the dressing ingredients in a blender and whiz to a puree.
3...Wash and dry the salad leaves.
4...Cut wafer thin slices from the beef with a very sharp knife. About 3oz-75gm per person.
5...Mix some of the dressing with the leaves and arrange them on plates. Cover the leaves with the wafer thin beef slices. Dribble a little extra dressing over the beef and sprinkle with the cracked black peppercorns. Sprinkle over shavings of parmesan cheese and snipped chives.

From the menu of...

GEE'S
61a Banbury Rd, Oxford OX2 6PE.   Tel:53540 Fax:310308
Proprietor: J Mogford
Chef: Graham Corbett
Open: All year. Monday-Saturday 12noon-2.30 and 6pm-11pm. Sunday 12noon-11pm.
Booking advised but casual callers welcome. Credit cards accepted. Children welcome.
Dine in their Victorian conservatory. Daily changing specials. Seafood, game and vegetarian dishes.

Light Lunches and Vegetarian Dishes

Most of the recipes in this section can be served either as a starter or a main course simply by increasing or decreasing the proportions. Because it is lunch and not a main meal of the day it is recommended that these recipes are served with a lightly dressed side salad.

Spiced Cranberry and Turkey Sandwich

Serve at Christmas for a festive flavour but just as tasty any time of year.

1lb-450gm cooked turkey (or chicken)
6 tbls mayonnaise
1 tspn curry powder
2 tbls cranberry sauce
½tspn English mustard
1 tbls double cream, optional
salt and pepper

1...Cut the turkey into bite sized pieces.
2...Beat together the remaining ingredients until smooth and evenly mixed.
3...Toss the turkey in the mayonnaise mixture.
4...Serve on plain Cibatta bread with a crisp salad garnish

One of the many choices from...

THE ALTERNATIVE TUCK SHOP
Sandwich Bar
24 Holywell Street, Oxford.   Tel:792054
Proprietor: Mr and Mrs Baker
Chef: Mrs Lesley Baker
Open: All year. 8.30am-6pm
Lots of vegetarian specials.

Little Game Pies

The game for this recipe can be obtained form the covered market

1lb-450gm shortcrust pastry: Made with 1lb-450gm plain flour, 10oz-275gm fat, 1 beaten egg and a drop of cold water

8oz-225gm pheasant or rabbit meat
8oz-225gm venison or hare meat
1 medium onion
1 small potato
½ tspn juniper berries
½ slice bread
salt and plenty of black pepper
1 tbls fresh sage, chopped
beaten egg for glazing

1...Make up the pastry and put to rest in the fridge.
2...Very finely chop the two meats. They can be briefly whizzed in the blender but don't make the meat too fine in texture.
3...Very finely chop the onion. Crush the juniper berries. Make breadcrumbs out of the bread. Mix these prepared ingredients together.
4...Add the chopped meat and fresh sage to the onion. Put in a covered bowl in the fridge for 1 hour for the flavours to blend.
5...Roll out the pastry and cut out circles with a 4" cutter. Lay half the circles on a rigid baking sheet. Place as much game mixture as you can in the centre of these pastry circles. Moisten the edges and press the second circle over the mixture to make a little dome. You may have to stretch the top circle of pastry slightly. Alternatively cut the top circles slightly larger. Cut a small slit in the top to allow steam to escape. Glaze with beaten egg. Bake in a pre-heated oven 200c/400f/gas6 for 15 minutes. Lower the temperature to 180c/350c/gas4 and cook for a further 20 minutes. Less if you prefer your meat on the pink side
Serve with red cabbage salad and Cumberland sauce or with seasonal vegetables and a game sauce.

N.B. This is also a good way to use up tough, old grouse.

Vegetarian Cookery

Vegetarianism has become an emotive subject, and a great deal of intolerance goes with it on both side of the argument. Of course there is no argument you either choose to be a vegetarian or not, and some vegetarians go further than others. This refusal to understand the vegetarian tends to blend with the few vegetarians who try to ram their beliefs down the throats of others. Their self-righteous attitude niggles, and 'those others' throw back strongly weighted questions that enter the grey areas of vegetarianism. It all causes considerable antagonism; when really we should be grateful we have the choice.

Nevertheless, there are more vegetarians in England today than ever, especially amongst the younger generation. They constitute four percent of the population and their needs are willingly recognized in cafes, restaurants and pubs all over the country. Not only that, it's not just an omelette any more, dishes have become creative and substantial, although understandably the choice is small. Some dishes have been so imaginatively conceived that even non-vegetarians will eat a vegetarian meal at lunch time.

There are advantages to vegetarian cookery. It is quick and easy, (no more waiting for the roast to cook) and it is highly suitable to microwave cookery. Vegetarian food is fresh tasting and full of roughage. The one thing it does lack is essential ascorbic acid, normally derived from meat, but it can be obtained from mushrooms.

Vegetarianism has to be approached sensibly. Vegetables, unlike meat and dairy produce have no protein which is essential for the development of the body, and if a vegetarian is involved in manual work the body needs to be strong. Protein can be obtained from nuts, but one nut to be carefully measured is coconut which has high cholesterol forming fats.

Pulses, pasta and pastry are great vehicles for vegetarian meals and the vegetables provide a colourful and tempting repast. There's also a wide variety of cheeses available for the less strict vegetarian, and many new ways of serving them other than just grated onto a bed of lettuce. In fact there is no shortage of ingredients available to ensure a healthy, interesting, tasty vegetarian diet.

Vegetarian Scotch Eggs

Most ingredients are available from Beanbag.

8 free range eggs
1 egg beaten
1 sachet of Sosmix (175gm)
5oz-150gm cheese, grated
1 medium onion, chopped
pinch each of pepper, herbamare, pizza herbs
½pt-275ml very cold water
wholemeal breadcrumbs
peanut oil for frying

1...Hard boil the eggs, for 10-12 minutes depending on size. Remove shells.
2...Mix together the sosmix, cheese, onion, pepper, herbamare, pizza herbs and water. Leave to stand for 10 minutes.
3...Divide the mixture and wrap around the eggs about a ¼" thick.
4...Dip in the beaten egg and breadcrumbs.
5...Heat the oil to very hot and deep fry the eggs for 10 minutes, turning after 5 minutes.
6...Drain on kitchen paper and serve warm or cold with salad.

Recipe supplied by...

BEANBAG WHOLEFOODS
48 High St, Witney, Oxon OX8 6HQ.   Tel: 01993 773922
Proprietor: Joan Bright
Chef: Jane Bright
Open: All year. 9am-5pm. Closed Christmas.
An essential shop for the healthy eater

The Herb Garden

The use of herbs in cookery goes as far back as the history of food has ever been recorded. For a long time tradition told us what herbs went best with which food. For example sage and onion stuffing with pork, mint sauce with lamb, tarragon with chicken, parsley with fish. However, as is always the case, things change, rules get broken and now, in the late twentieth century the domestic kitchen has become a huge laboratory of experimentation. Herb cookery is all over the place as we try swopping around the flavours, some old, others quite new to us. Modern English cookery is mixing, for example, French cookery with Indian cookery, and Thai cookery with English cookery; It is all very exciting.

Gardeners too are paying more attention to the flavourings, finding larger corners to grow their garden of herbs amongst the rows of vegetables. The old tradition of a knot garden made from fragrant herbs is beginning to form a small oasis in the modern ornamental garden.

There are numerous herb specialists in the country. As far as I know the nearest one to Oxford is Hollington Herb Garden at Newbury. They have in the past won the gold medal at Chelsea Flower show. There is a retail nursery and herb shop. Cookery demonstrations from time to time. A display garden for inspiration and a tearoom which is open all summer for the thirsty.

Pesto Sauce.

2 cups fresh basil
½ cup fresh parsley
½ cup olive oil
1 tbls pine nuts
1 tspn salt
½ cup grated Parmesan cheese

Puree together in a blender the first five ingredients. Then stir in the cheese. It's as simple as that! Best used fresh with pasta or as a salsa to go with fish or meat.
It will keep in the fridge for three days.

Pizza Tart 1990

Individual tarts can also be made from this recipe

6 sheets filo pastry
olive oil
1 red pepper
1 green pepper
1 yellow pepper
2 beefsteak tomatoes
1 red onion, sliced
3 cloves garlic, cut into thin slivers
1 tbls capers
small bunch fresh basil leaves
4oz-110gm mozarellas cheese
2oz-50gm fresh Parmesan cheese, in one piece
1 tbls tomato puree

1 Cut the peppers into quarters. Brush the skins with olive oil and grill skin side up until they start to go black. Cover with a tea-towel while removing the charred skins. Put to one side.
2 Brush the filo sheets with olive oil and use the sheets to line a 10inch-25cm shallow flan ring.
3 Spread the tomato paste over the base of the flan ring. Tear up some basil leaves and scatter over the tomato puree. Cut the mozarellas into thin slivers and scatter on top. Slice the tomatoes and arrange on top of the cheese. Scatter over more torn basil and the slivers of garlic. Now scatter over the prepared quarters of peppers and red onion slices.
4 Finnish off with any left over mozarellas cheese and a scattering of capers. Place in a hot oven gas7/425f/220c and bake for 20-30 minutes.
5 Remove from the oven. Shave the Parmesan into wafer thin curls with a potato peeler and scatter over the pizza tart. Serve with a simple dressed salad. Serves 4.

Primavera

Fasta Pasta's quick and easy variation on a traditional sauce full of Spring-time character. Virtually all the ingredients for this recipe are available at Fasta Pasta, including occasionally, fresh porcini mushrooms (ceps), which can be used instead of dried porcini.

4oz-110gm courgettes, sliced
4 artichoke hearts
3oz-75gm fresh peas
¼oz-5gm dried porcini mushrooms
3oz-75gm cherry tomatoes
9fl oz-250ml fresh cream
12oz-350gm fresh pasta, pappardelle or tagliatelle

1...First prepare the vegetables. If using fresh artichokes prepare them in the following way. Peel the outer leaves until you reach the softer outer leaves inside. Turn the artichoke upside-down and pare off the stem by cutting around the stem and slightly into the base. Turn it round and cut off the top. Open the leaves out with your fingers and cut out the hairy 'choke'. Plunge the artichokes into a mixture of water and lemon juice to maintain their colour. When all the artichokes are ready, cut into quarters.
2...Soak the dried mushrooms, either for 30 minutes in very hot water or for several hours in red wine. Keep the resulting stock.
3...Slowly cook the quartered artichoke hearts in a little butter for approximately 10 minutes. Add the sliced courgettes followed by the procini mushrooms, with some of their stock. Reduce the stock then turn down the heat. Season to taste. Add the cream and heat gently. Finally add the peas and cherry tomatoes, cook for a further minute or two.
4...Meanwhile, boil a large pan filled with salted water (the more water pasta is cooked in the better it will taste). Plunge the fresh pasta into the water and boil for the recommended amount of time. (Staff at Fasta Pasta will advice customers on cooking times). Strain the pasta and rinse under boiling water. Pour some good quality olive oil over the top and toss together.

5...Return the pasta to the large pan, pour the sauce on top and toss the two together.
6...Serve with freshly shaved Parmigiano Reggiano (high quality parmesan) and some cracked pepper. Serves 4 people.

Recipe supplied by…

FASTA PASTA
121 The Covered Market, Oxford, OX1 3DZ.   Tel: 01865 241973
Proprietor: Ailsa
Open: Monday - Saturday 9am-5.30pm and Sundays over Christmas.
Italian delicatessen. Purveyors of fresh pasta, fresh sauces and salads and traditional Italian groceries. Delicious and authentic ciabatta bread which won the best bread of Britain award from Henrietta Green.

Mushroom and Courgette Loaf

1 large onion
1½oz-40gm melted butter
1 clove garlic, minced
1 pinch dried basil or sage
1 dssrt spn tamari or soy sauce
1 dssrt spn chopped, fresh, parsley
1lb-450gm courgettes
8oz-225gm mushrooms
4oz-110gm strong cheese
wholemeal breadcrumbs
salt and pepper to taste
Topping: 2oz-50gm grated cheddar cheese and 3oz-75gm wholemeal breadcrumbs

1...Cook the chopped onion in the butter until transparent.
2...Add the garlic, herbs, tamari, salt and pepper. Be wary of the salt as the tamari has quite a lot.
3...Grate the courgettes and chop the mushrooms. Add to the onions. Mix thoroughly and cook gently for 4 minutes. Add the strong cheese and breadcrumbs.
4...Lightly press the mixture into a baking dish. Sprinkle with the cheese and wholemeal breadcrumb topping then bake in pre-heated oven, 190c/375f/gas5 until the top is brown.

Serve warm with salad garnish.

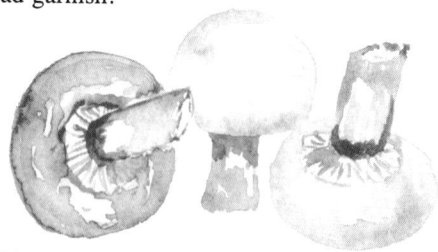

From the kitchen of...

CAFE MOMA
30 Pembroke St, Oxford OX1 BPI. Tel:01865 722733 Fax:722573
Proprietors: Museum of Modern Art
Chefs: Mains, Sam Mason. Salads, Helena Newsom. Pastries and cakes Catherine Frew and Kate Glanville.
Casual callers and children welcome. Wheelchair access.
A cafe that offers an extensive vegetarian menu and an emphasis on home-made everything!

Oxford Baked Egg

A simple and delicious dish using the best dairy produce and Oxford's very own Blue Cheese which has the sharpness of a Danish blue but the full roundness of a Stilton.

4 size 1 eggs
2 small or 1 large leek, thinly sliced and softened in butter
8 tbls double cream, (approx) must be double
6oz-175gm Oxford Blue, (be generous)
salt and pepper

1...Pre-heat oven to its highest setting
2...Divide the leeks between four large cocotte dishes leaving a hollow in the centre.
3...Break 1 egg in the centre of each hollow, then sprinkle over generous amounts of grated Oxford Blue.
4...Spoon over the double cream 2-3 tbls per cocotte.
5...Place the cocottes on a baking tray and put in the oven for 15-20 minutes depending how well you like your eggs done.
To serve: put a folded napkin on a plate and serve immediately. Garnish with a sprig of fresh herbs.

Variations - smoked haddock, cooked smoked ham, sautéd mushrooms, cooked spinach, chopped tomatoes, prawns, left over bolognaise. Topped with: Stilton cheese, cheddar or smoked cheddar, goats milk cheese, roqueforte cheese, emmental and gruyer cheese.

Pumpkin and Leek Risotto

Approx 3oz-75gm arborio rice per person
1 medium sized butternut squash, approx 1lb-450gm
2 small leeks
1 small onion, finely chopped
1 clove garlic, crushed
1 stock cube
bay leaves
2oz-50gm reggiano parmesan
8oz-225gm fresh spinach
4oz-110gm pancetta
salt and pepper
olive oil

1...Chop the pumpkin into small pieces. Boil until soft with the bay leaves, salt, pepper and stock cube.
2...Fry the leeks, onion and garlic in a little olive oil in a very large pan. Add the arborio rice. Stir to make sure the rice is well coated with oil. Let it gently fry for a couple of minutes.
3...When the pumpkin is soft and the water takes on a 'stock' appearance, add it to the rice mixture - a ladle at a time. Let the rice soak up the stock and soft pumpkin by stirring gently.
4...When all the stock and pumpkin is absorbed into the rice cook gently until swelled and soft. Finally add the freshly grated parmesan cheese.
5...Meanwhile, fry the pancetta in a pan. When slightly crisp add the fresh spinach leaves and cook until the spinach is soft.
6...To serve. Place the risotto onto hot plates and top with the spinach and pancetta.

Recipe supplied by...

FASTA PASTA
121 The Covered Market, Oxford, OX1 3DZ.   Tel: 01865 241973
Proprietor: Ailsa Ward
Open: Monday - Saturday 9am-5.30pm and Sundays over Christmas.
Italian delicatessen. Purveyors of fresh pasta, fresh sauces and salads and traditional Italian groceries. Stock delicious and authentic ciabatta bread which won the best bread of Britain award from Henrietta Green.

The Perfect Quiche Lorraine (egg and bacon flan)

Soggy bottoms and undercooked vegetables are the most common signs of an imperfect quiche. Yet if performed correctly this should never happen. As with all good dishes, perfection doesn't come easily. Corners can't be cut, despite modern life and lack of time, it has to be done properly and laboriously.

Pastry: 6oz-175gm plain flour; 2oz-50gm lard (cookeen); 2oz-50gm butter or hard margarine; 3 tbls cold water; ½ tspn salt
Filling
1 medium onion finely chopped
4 rashers smoked bacon
2 large or 3 small eggs
½pt-275ml milk
2 tbls cream
salt and pepper
4oz-110gm mature cheddar

1...Mix the flour and salt together then rub in the two fats. Add the water, a little at a time, and bind the mixture together. Wrap the pastry in cling film and put in the fridge for 20 minutes to relax.
2...Remove the pastry from the fridge and roll out to a size large enough to line a 7"-18cm diameter flan ring. Not too thin though. Fit the pastry so that it stands ¼"-0.5cm above the ring. This will allow for shrinkage. Lightly prick the centre of the flan and line the bottom and sides with tin foil. Weigh down the centre with baking beans or bread. Place in a pre-heated oven 220c/425f/gas7 and bake for 15 minutes. Remove the bread/beans and tin foil. Lower the temperature of the oven to 180c/325f/gas4 and bake the flan for a further 10 minutes to dry out the bottom of the flan. Some people think they can get away with not blind baking the flan first. To compensate they have to cook the quiche at a high temperature for a longer time so that the pastry crisps up. This means that the custard filling will bubble up and separate.
3...While the flan is being blind-baked prepare the filling. Soften the onions in a little oil. Grill the bacon and snip into small pieces. Beat the eggs with the milk and cream and add the grated cheddar.
4...Sprinkle the softened onion and cooked bacon over the base of the partly cooked flan. Pour over the egg mixture leaving a space at the top of ¼"-0.5cm. It is essential that you don't over fill the flan. Return to the oven and bake 180c/350f/gas4 for 35-40 minutes.

Vegetarian Lasagne

A traditional tasty pub recipe made special by the addition of red wine.

12oz-350gm puy lentils
1 large onion chopped
2 tbls oil
1 hpd tspn each dried oregano, ground cumin, ground coriander
2 tbls black olives, stoned and chopped
3 or 4 cloves garlic crushed with a little salt
½pt red wine
4 sticks celery, chopped
1 tin Italian chopped tomatoes
½ small tin tomato puree
salt and pepper
Cheese Sauce - 1oz-25gm flour, 1oz-25gm butter plus 1 tbls oil, good ½pt-275ml milk, 6oz-175gm mature cheddar
12 sheets dried lasagne pasta.
4 fresh tomatoes

1...Heat the oil in a frying pan and cook the celery, onion and garlic until golden. Add the puy lentils, red wine, oregano and cumin and cook until soft and almost dry. Add tinned tomatoes, tomato puree, and seasoning and simmer gently for thirty minutes until the mixture reduces and becomes thicker.
2...Meanwhile make the cheese sauce. Melt the butter and oil in a saucepan and add the flour. Cook for one minute without browning. Add the milk and stir all the time until the sauce thickens. Grate the cheese and add 4oz-110gm to the sauce. Cook gently until the cheese has melted.
3...Spread some of the lentil mixture over the bottom of an oblong casserole dish. Top with three pasta sheets. Continue until the lentils and pasta is used up. End with a pasta sheet.
4...Pour the cheese sauce over the pasta. Arrange sliced tomato on top and sprinkle over remaining cheese. (If the pasta is not the easy to use type, let the dish stand for thirty minutes so that the sauce begins to soften the pasta.) Bake in a pre-heated oven. 200c/400f/gas 6 for 20-30 minutes until the top is golden brown and bubbling. Serve with crusty bread, green salad.

Sesame Rabbit Salad

This dish can also be served as a starter

4 saddles of hutch rabbit
2 rashers smoked streaky bacon, diced
4 tbls sesame seeds
2 pink or ruby grapefruits, separated into segments
selection of salad leaves
½ a celeriac, peeled and cut into matchsticks
2 tbls soured cream
oil for frying
Dressing
3 tbls salad oil
1 tbls smoked sesame oil
1 tbls white wine vinegar
2 tspns runny honey
1 tspn whole grain mustard

1...Blanch the celeriac in boiling water until just tender. refresh and chill. Mix with the soured cream, season to taste. Put to one side.
2...Arrange a nest of salad leaves and grapefruit segments onto four plates. Pile a spoonful of celeriac in the middle of each nest of leaves.
3...Cut the rabbit saddles into ½"-0.5cm thick medallions. Toss in the sesame seeds to coat liberally. Heat the oil in a pan and add the bacon, Fry for a few minutes then add the rabbit pieces and saute over a medium heat until golden brown.
4...Whisk together the dressing ingredients.
4...Arrange on the salad leaves with the by now crispy bits of bacon and spoon over the dressing. Serve while the rabbit is still hot.

Oxford Brawn Sauce

This is an old traditional recipe so presumably good malt vinegar was used. As well as with brawn this sauce is good with sausages and vegetable terrines such as leek. Expert cooks will of course recognise this recipe as a salad dressing.

2 tbls brown sugar
2 tspns English made mustard
¼ tspn salt
scant ¼ tspn white pepper
8 tbls good quality salad oil i.e grape seed
4 tbls vinegar

1...Mix the dry ingredients together.
2...Blend in the oil and made mustard
3...Add the vinegar

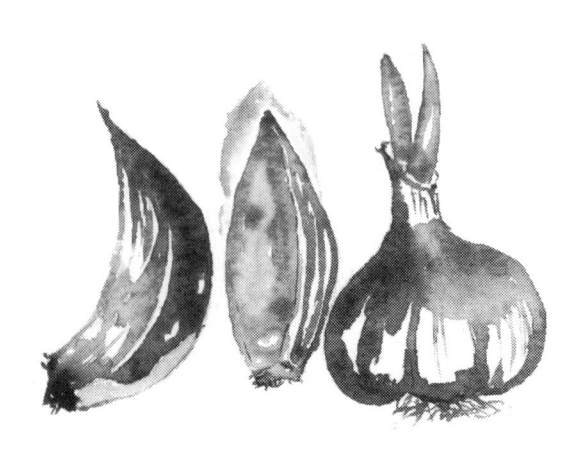

Stroff's Vegetarian Sausage with Hazelnut Oil and Lemon Dressing

The joy of Stroff's sausages is that they are a meal on their own. However each one can also add something special to a composite meal.

2 spinach, apricot and smoked tofu sausages per person
handful of mixed salad leaves per person
½ tbls freshly squeezed lemon juice
1 tbls hazelnut oil
salt and pepper

1...Pan fry or bake the sausages until the hazelnut coating is crispy.
2...Meanwhile, take a handful of salad leaves and toss in the lemon juice and hazelnut oil.
3...Make a nest with the leaves on the plate and arrange the hot crispy sausages on top.

Stroff's Seafood Boudin with Mangetout and Herb Butter Sauce

8 seafood boudin
2 shallots
½pt-275ml white wine
4oz-110gm butter
2 tbls chopped fresh herbs i.e. dill, tarragon, parsley, basil
12oz-350gm mange tout
1 tbls chopped fresh tomato concasse
1 tbls lemon juice
salt and pepper
Serves 4.

1...Cook the seafood sausages as directed; in the microwave oven is quickest.
2...Meanwhile, finely chop the shallots and soften in a little butter and water.
3...Once cooked keep the boudin warm and gently pour the fish stock that comes with it on to the shallots. Add the white wine and bring to the boil briefly.
4...Off the heat whisk in the butter until the sauce is emulsified. Add the freshly chopped herbs.
5...While you are making the sauce steam the mangetout.
6...To finish the sauce add the chopped tomato, lemon juice and seasoning and heat gently. Do not boil otherwise the butter will separate from the liquid. Pour the sauce around the sausages and serve with the mange tout.

Stroff's Sicilian Sausage with Pasta

8 Sicilian sausages
1 onion, finely chopped
2 carrots, small dice
2 sticks celery, thinly sliced
8oz-225gm chopped fresh tomatoes
1 tin chopped plum tomatoes
salt, pepper and pinch of sugar
pasta for 4 people
fresh basil leaves for garnish

1...Pan fry the sausages until nicely browned. Set aside.
2...In the same pan soften the chopped onion, diced carrot and sliced celery until golden brown. Add the salt, pepper and sugar. Then add the fresh and tinned tomatoes. Cook gently until the sauce begins to thicken.
3...Put the pasta on to cook. Tip: Place the pasta in cold water at the beginning of preparing the sauce. Cover with a lid. Bring to the boil, then turn off the heat. Keep the lid firmly on. By the time you have finished the sauce the pasta will have cooked in the residual heat.
4...Cut the sausages into bite sized pieces and add to the sauce. Simmer until heated through.
5...Drain the pasta. Pour over the sauce and garnish with torn basil leaves. Serves 4.

Recipes supplied by...

STROFF'S SPECIALITY SAUSAGES
96 The Covered Market, Oxford OX1 3DY.   Tel:01865 200922
Proprietors: Simon Offen and David Walker
Sausage Maker: Simon Offen
Open: All year. 8.30am-5pm. Closed Christmas and New Year
Stroff's offer an enormous range of delicious sausages. Own label condiments.
They use local pork reared outside for quality and flavour, and only natural skins. Also vegetarian and seafood sausages.
Oxford, Cumberland, Cajun, Toulouse, Duck and Orange, Venison, Mushroom and Tarragon, Fish Provencale to name just a few from their seasonally changing menu.

Fish and Shellfish

Fish is highly nutritious and healthy as well as being low in saturated fats. When shopping always try to buy the whole fish rather than fillets or steaks. That way you can see what sort of condition it is in. Generally speaking, eyes should be bright and slightly protruding. The scales tend to come off ultra fresh fish easily. Its body should be firm, almost stiff, definitely not floppy. White fish should smell of the sea and not at all "fishy".

At home we tend to avoid serving fish both as a starter and main course, yet if you go to a seafood restaurant this is difficult to avoid. As long as the type of fish used and the sauce served have different characteristics, there's nothing wrong with serving fish twice.

Fillet of Cod with Claytonia and Tomato Dressing

4 x 6-7oz-200gm fillet of cod
1 tbls oil
2oz-50gm butter
1lb claytonia (from Halcyon Herbs)
1 level tbls tomato puree
6 tomatoes, chopped
3-4 shallots, chopped
8 fl oz white wine
8 fl oz fish stock
8fl oz virgin olive oil
1 lemon
salt and pepper
2 fl oz balsamic vinegar
2 tspn curly chervil

1...Heat oil in a heavy pan. When hot add the butter.
2...Season the cod fillets and saute skin side uppermost. When brown turn over and cook for 2 minutes on the other side. Remove from the pan.
3...Saute the claytonia for 10 seconds. Add squeeze of lemon juice, salt and pepper. Divide between 4 warm plates. Arrange the cod fillets on top and keep warm.
4...Add the shallot to the pan and saute until soft. Add tomato puree and cook out. Deglaze with white wine and stock. Add the chopped tomatoes and boil down by half. Pass thorough a fine sieve into a clean pan.
5...Combine the extra virgin oil with the tomato mixture. Bring to the boil. Season with lemon juice, salt and pepper and a little balsamic vinegar. Add chopped chervil. Pour sauce around the cod, garnish with chervil sprigs. Serves 4 people.

From the kitchen of...

GEE'S
61a Banbury Rd, Oxford OX2 6PE. Tel:53540 Fax:310308
Proprietor: J Mogford
Chef: Graham Corbett
Open: All year. Monday-Saturday 12noon-2.30 and 6pm-11pm. Sunday 12noon-11pm.
Booking advised but casual callers welcome. Credit cards accepted. Children welcome.
Dine in their Victorian conservatory. Daily changing specials. Seafood, game and vegetarian dishes.

Oxford Waterways

Study a map of the city of Oxford and you would soon begin to see the city as an Island. Down the east of the city flows the river Cherwell and around from the wests flows Englands most famous river, the Thames. From these two rivers stem capillaries of smaller rivers and streams, weaving in and out of the city and creating a network of waterways.

At one time the waterways were a major form of industrial transport to many parts of the country. But as with most water ways in the country they were superseded by the more direct and faster motorways. Both the Thames and the Cherwell are now considered waterways for leisure.

One of the best things that happened to Englands rivers in recent times is the National Rivers Authority, which took over all rivers when water was privatised. Their job is to prevent problems of pollution and to generally clean up the standard of water in the Thames which in turn encourages the wild life population, the fresh water fish and plant life that live in the rivers.

Angling is greatly controlled these days and most fishermen will need to belong to an angling club of which there are a good many in the area.

Thanks to the work of the NRA and the controls on fishing, stocks of fresh water fish are growing and a meal of freshly caught fish is once again becoming a more regular occurrence.

The Thames supports virtually every species found in the country. Gourmets will be pleased to be able to buy at local fish mongers, pike and brown trout which in the eighties became a prize to find.

In 1974 there was an exciting discovery of an adult salmon, the first in 150 years; suggesting that the river water might once again be clean enough to support its passage. The Thames water authority set up a rehabilitation programme.

During the month of June elvers swim up river from the Sargasso sea and return there in October and November.

There are many, many more species of fish than those mentioned above, but there is little doubt that a feast of fish can taken from the river. However it must be noted that can be caught only by approved methods, under the NRA, Thames Region, bylaws.

Baked Salmon with Sorrel Sauce

2lb-900gm fillet of salmon
salt and pepper
4 pinches Chinese five spice powder
4 knobs butter
4 sprigs of fresh fennel, dill or chervil
<u>Sauce</u>
6 sorrel leaves
2 shallots, skinned and quartered
¼pt-150ml strong fish stock
¼pt-150ml white wine
½pt-275ml whipping cream
1oz-25gm butter

1...First prepare the sauce. Place in a large heavy bottomed saucepan (aluminium or stainless steel) the fish stock, white wine, sorrel leaves and shallots. Simmer slowly until the shallots are very soft. Blend until smooth. Return to the saucepan and add the cream. Bring to the boil and simmer until the sauce thickens.
2...Remove the skin from the salmon fillet and cut into four portions. Grease a baking tray and lay on the salmon fillets. Smear a knob of butter on top of each fillet and lay on top the sprigs of chosen herb then sprinkle with the salt, pepper and Chinese five spice powder. Put in a pre-heated oven 220c/425f/gas7 and bake for 10 minutes.
3...Meanwhile re-heat the sauce. Add the butter to enrich the sauce. Adjust the seasoning.
4...Arrange the salmon fillets on warm plates and pour over some of the sauce. Serve with new potatoes, French beans and braised fennel.

Pan Fried Brown Trout with Parsley Butter

4 brown trout
flour
4 tbls oil
4oz-110gm butter
juice of half a lemon
2 or 3 tbls white wine
2oz-50gm freshly chopped parsley
salt and plenty of black pepper

1...Clean and de-scale the trout. Remove heads if wished. Lightly toss in flour and shake off the surplus.
2...Heat the oil in a large frying pan that will take all the trout. When the oil is hot lay in the trout and fry over a medium heat about 8 minutes each side. Transfer the trout from the pan to a serving dish and keep warm in a low oven. They will in fact continue to cook in their own heat.
3...Add the wine, lemon juice, parsley and butter to the pan in which the trout has been cooked and cook over a high heat until the flavours have amalgamated and a pale buttery sauce has formed. Pour over the trout and serve immediately.
Serve simply with brown bread and butter and a warm salad of beans and mange tout.

Meat, Poultry and Game

A menu is often designed around the meat or main course so this is probably the easiest dish to decide upon. It is best to make your choice depending upon seasonal availability. For example, game in the Autumn, poultry and pork at Christmas, lamb in Spring and early Summer, and beef, once the most popular of meats but less so now that red meat has lost favour with the healthies, is available all year round.

Meat is less fatty these days, which is a great shame since most of the flavour is carried in the fat. It is much better to eat and enjoy a good flavoursome, fatty, roast, but less often than you would a fatless, tasteless roast.

These days meat is sold ultra fresh, which invariably means it hasn't been hung unless it has been through the hands of a good traditional family butcher. Meat is hung to improve the flavour and tenderness.

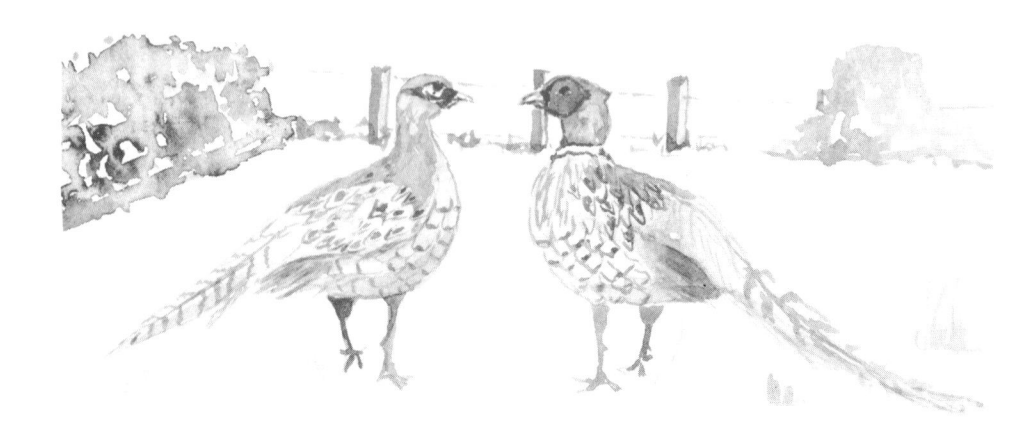

Stifatho
(Beef and onion stew)

2lb-900gm chuck steak, diced
1lb 8oz-700gm shallots, or onions if shallots not available
2 fl oz-50ml red wine vinegar
4 fl oz-100ml robust red wine
2 tspns demerara sugar
1 tspn tomato paste
1 clove garlic, crushed
3-4 dried bay leaves
salt and pepper
½ tspn cinnamon powder
½ tspn cumin powder
2 fl oz-50ml olive oil, or corn oil

1...Brown the meat in the hot oil. Do this in batches. Put to one side.
2...In the same pan brown the shallots or onions. Add the cinnamon, cumin, salt and pepper. Stir in and cook for 2 minutes.
3...Return the meat to the pan and add the rest of the ingredients. Bring to the boil then cover the pot and simmer gently for approximately 45 minutes or until the meat is tender. Do not over cook or the flavour of the meat will be lost in the rich sauce.
4...Serve with pilaf rice or parsley potatoes. Serves 4 people.

From the menu of...

GREEK TAVERNA
272 Banbury Rd, Summertown, Oxford OX2 7DY   Tel: 01865 511472
Proprietor: Nicholas G Paplomatas
Chef: Mr B Novin
Open: All year. Lunch Tues-Sat 12noon-2pm. Dinner Mon-Sat 6.30-11am
Casual callers and children welcome. Credit cards accepted. Wheelchair access. Seafood and vegetarian dishes. Specialises in Greek and Cypriot food.

Old Speckled Hen Beef

Old Speckled Hen is a cask beer brewed just outside Oxford

top side joint of beef approx 3-4lb/1.4-1.8kg
1 bottle of Old Speckled Hen
3 tbls seasoned flour
2 carrots
2 medium onions
2 cloves garlic
2 sticks celery
1 tspn black peppercorns
4 cloves
oil

1...Peel and finely chop the onions. Scrape and finely chop the carrots. Cut the celery into thin slices.
2...Heat some oil in a roasting tin and add the vegetables, garlic cloves, cloves and peppercorns. Stir fry the vegetables until they begin to colour. Push to one side of the tin.
3...Generously coat the topside joint in seasoned flour. Add a drop more oil to the roasting tin if necessary. Brown the joint on all sides.
4...Spread the vegetables back over the base of the roasting tin and position the joint on top. Pour the Old Speckled Hen around the joint. Loosely over with tin foil and pot-roast in a pre-heated oven 190c/375f/gas6 for 1 hour. Occasionally baste the meat with the beer during this time. After 1 hour Remove the tin foil and continue roasting for a further 20 minutes - more or less depending on the size of the joint and how well done you like your meat.
5...Remove the meat from the pan and keep warm. Put the roasting pan with the stock and vegetables over the stove. Stir thoroughly and boil rapidly to reduce the sauce to a rich glaze. (If you wish add a tspn of tomato puree).
6...Thinly slice the beef and serve with the sauce, English mustard, carrots and creamed potatoes, or for a more modern touch with thick tagliatelle.

The Value of Meat

More than anything it is important to eat a balanced diet, yet because of the bad, sometimes uninformed publicity over recent years more people have ceased to eat meat - therefore, unbalancing their diet.

Meat is extremely good for you and meat products in general, such as milk and eggs are essential for a healthy diet. If you cut them out as vegans do then artificial substitutes have to be taken to replace lost nutriments.

Looking at it scientifically the body needs the building blocks of protein which are amino acids. The body is unable to manufacture these acids so it has to get them from 'high-quality' protein which is found in meat. Protein is essential to everyone but particularly to children who have fast growing bodies. The body also needs vitamin B12 and meat products are virtually the only dietary source: plant foods lack vitamin B12.

Minerals are also important. Iron, it is true is available in grains, nuts and pulses (via baked products) but by far the best source is meat, simply because it is chemically bound to the blood-protein haemoglobin and is therefore, rapidly absorbed into the blood. This is not the case with iron found in plants and lack of iron can cause anaemia.

The amount of meat required for a healthy diet depends on whether you are male or female, a pregnant woman or a growing child, the last two. by the way need the most. The average person within these categories requires 6-9 oz of meat (or fish) per day. We are not talking 16oz T Bone steaks here but a few slices of roast beef or an average sized chicken breast.

Unbeknown to many people, most meat is reared in happy conditions. Fields full of cows (beef) and sheep (lamb) is proof of that, and in fact have always been reared that way; and these days it is not uncommon to see pigs rooting around in the open fields. Battery chicken do still exist and are very cheap, but for a little extra money you can easily purchase a free range chicken. The more of you that do, the more common and eventually cheaper free range chickens (and eggs) will become.

It is not in the farmer's interest not to look after his animals unless he wants to fork out money for hefty vets bills, and an animal that has been stressed in the slaughter house, as so many people claim, results in inedible meat, what's the point of that!

In the same way that a damaged apple is inedible so is damaged meat and great care is taken that this should not happen. At least the meat you eat has not been sprayed with insecticide and if an animal is ill the antibiotics it is given to help its recovery are no more harmful than the ones the doctor gives us to aid our own recovery.

Meat is essential for the development of strong healthy children and very important to people in active work, be it for pleasure or pay.

Lamb Boulangere

This recipe is very representative of St Aldates varied menu.

1lb-450gm lamb cutlets
2lb-900gm onions, sliced
5lb-150gm potatoes
fresh herbs, rosemary, thyme or parsley or mixed dried herbs
2-3pts-1.1-1.75ml meat stock
salt and pepper
oil for browning

1...Seal the lamb cutlets in hot oil with the herbs and a quarter of the onions.
2...Place in a deep oven-proof dish. Pour over the stock and season.
3...Scatter the remaining onions over the cutlets.
4...Peel and slice the potatoes and arrange them on top of the onions.
5...Brush with melted butter then cook in a moderate oven 180c/350f/gas4 for 1hr-1hr 15 minutes.
Serve with peas and glazed carrots.

From the menu of...

ST ALDATES COFFEE HOUSE
94 St Aldates, Oxford OX1 1BP. Tel: 01865 245952
Proprietor: St Aldates P.C.C.
Chefs: Ron Binder and Nick Sutton
Open: Winter 9.30-5pm and Summer 9.30-5.30. Closed 23rd Dec-4th Jan
Casual callers and children welcome. Outside seating in Summer. 10% discount to all students with I.D.
Fresh, homemade dishes. Varied menu including, English, French and Asian styles.

Colcannon

A recipe to go with many braised meat dishes.

3lb-1.4kg scrubbed potatoes
1 medium head of cabbage, finely shredded
1 onion, finely chopped
½pt-275ml milk
salt and black pepper
4oz-110gm butter

1...Boil the potatoes until tender. Then drain and remove the skins.
2...Boil the shredded cabbage in a separate pan.
3...Gently cook the onion in the milk.
4...Mash the potatoes with the milk and onion then add the cooked cabbage and the butter. Mash well. Season with black pepper and salt and Serve.
Serves 6 people.

A Hygienic Kitchen

Healthy eating starts before you do the shopping and doesn't have an awful lot to do with the kind of food you eat!

Anyone involved in the catering industry is already acutely aware of the importance of strict hygiene. Not only because of the threat of closure if the Health Inspector isn't satisfied with standards, but because they have no desire to make their paying customers ill.

A health inspector would probably reel back in horror if invited to inspect a domestic kitchen as would its owner if they knew just how stiff the regulations were.

Out would go the cat, the dog, their baskets, their bowls of food and water and their owners coats, shoes and handbags. The beautifully carved chopping board would have to be burned, and all those little bits of sauce, too good to waste and shoved to the back of the fridge would definitely be out the door. Smoking would have to be banned and so would anyone with a cough or cold. In fact anything remotely considered a carrier of germs no matter how small would have to go. Even the wedding ring and not just for the washing up!

If an inspector looked into the average domestic fridge he might just die of fright! Uncovered food, raw meat next to cooked meat, temperature not cold enough, ice box 'iced-up'. Indeed the fridge will probably be in the wrong place anyway. Next to the cooker, washing machine or in direct sunlight. All of which will help to lower the temperature.

Then there's the cleaning. Mopping the floor and wiping the worksurfaces every day is not enough. Anywhere that dust and grease can congregate to provide luxury accommodation for crawling insects - that get into mischief in the night - must be kept spotlessly clean. For the caterer this means pulling out fridges, freezers, washing machines and cookers and thoroughly cleaning behind them at least once a week. Walls, windows, door frames and light fittings must all be clean, and if you've got a dirty oven, the worst job of all, you'll get a sever rap on the knuckles.

Such extremes of cleanliness in a domestic kitchen which more often t resembles Picadilly station, is almost possible to adhere to. However, a few simple and sensible rules are worth considering.

PETS: It's impossible to keep pets out of the kitchen. The smell of food is too compelling, it's probably their favourite room in the house. Train your dog at an early age not to jump up to sniff counters and cats not to walk over them. This may be more difficult if bad habits have already developed. If this is the case be a little more rigorous with your cleaning. Just before commencing work wipe the surface with disinfectant. (Clear dettol is ideal).

DISH CLOTHS, TEATOWELS AND WASTE BINS: All wonderful sanctuaries for germs. If you have used a dish cloth to wipe up blood from raw meat, wash it thoroughly before using it again or use kitchen roll. Use a clean teatowel every day and don't be tempted to dry your hands on it. Ideally wash dishes in water that is too hot to put your bare

hands in (protect them with rubber gloves) then let the plates drip dry. Waste bins should be covered at all times to deter flies, a species that has an acute sense of smell.
FRIDGES: Store raw meat, i.e. sausages, bacon, gammon steaks, joints of meat, chicken and barbecue meat in spices in a plastic container kept specially for this job.
   You might be surprised to know that the warmest part of the fridge is next to the ice box (warm air rises, remember!?). You could buy a cheap thermometer from the supermarket and keep it on the top shelf and use as a guide. Never put warm or hot food straight into the fridge as this raises the temperature and reduces effectiveness. Also don't leave the fridge door open when, for instance getting the milk out, it only takes a second for the cold air to rush out and hot air in.
FREEZERS: Freezing does not kill bacteria's. Bacteria's only remains dormant when frozen and indeed some bacteria's, such as listeria can still grow, albeit slowly. Don't freeze food for too long as it can deteriorate, although this might not necessarily be harmful. Keep a track of when you put food in the freezer and always cover food to be frozen otherwise it could suffer from freezer burn which can destroy the texture of food.
HYGIENE: Always wash your hands after handling raw meat.
   Naturally you must always wash your hands after using the toilet. It is essential that young children, who love to suck their fingers, learn this habit. It is very easy to pass nasty germs onto plates touched by contaminated hands.
VERMIN: If you live in the country you can be troubled with infestations of mice and rats, and in the town cockroaches as well as rats. Then there is the continuous troop of flies, flour beetles and silver fish. Ideally keep food off the ground in high cupboards. Keep everything well sealed and don't leave food lying around as a tempting midnight feast. Even a crumb of bread on the floor will be an attraction. And believe me it doesn't take long for the word to get around. Ants are particularly good at communications.
   If you have a serious problem contact the public health who have a department that can deal quite efficiently with these unwanted guests.
SHOPPING: Be wary and keep your eyes open. Do the staff look scruffy, dangling hair, bare hands at meat counters. Blowing their nose. Dirty floors and counters and dirty toilets in pubs and restaurants should all make you suspicious of their standards of hygiene.
FRESH FRUIT: Is often hand picked and not always washed afterwards. Strawberries may for instance may have been picked by contaminated hands, yours or someone else's. Therefore wash all fruits and salads before consuming.
PARANOIA: It is right that people in the catering trade should be paranoid about hygiene, their livelihood is at stake.
   But we should be more relaxed. All my life I have eaten raw eggs, rare meat, well hung game, under-cooked pork and even food that has been in and out of the freezer a couple of times and have never had food poisoning as a result.
   Some people are of the school of thought that too much hygiene is bad for us. 'Death by Hygiene' may not seem such a funny idea if the body is not allowed to build up a certain resistance to some common bacteria's and germs, and too much hygiene will make sure of that.

Carre d'Agneau Provencale

Best end of Spring lamb coated with a herb-scented crust.
From Raymond Blanc's book 'Cooking For Friends' published by Hodder Headline.

Although it's said that spring lamb is best, this recipe can also be done in the Summer or early Autumn. Raymond finds that Summer lamb is best (around 6 months old), when it has a powerful yet subtle flavour. This main-course dinner party dish with its Provencal overtones will bring the sunshine to your table. Serve with a fragrant Provencal red wine such as Domaine de la Bernarde.
For 4 guests.
2 best ends of spring lamb, about 8 ribs, perfectly trimmed
2 tbls olive oil
salt and freshly ground pepper
4 lamb bones, to use as a stand for the meat
1 tbls Dijon mustard
For the juice:
11oz-300gm reserved lamb bones, chopped into small pieces
2 tbls olive oil
¼ onion, peeled and chopped
1 garlic clove, unpeeled
1 tiny sprig rosemary
4 sprig of thyme
3½ fl oz-100ml dry white wine
1 tspn tomato puree
14 fl oz-400ml water
Lamb coating:
4oz-100gm dried breadcrumbs
4 tbls chopped fresh parsley
1 tspn dried chopped thyme
a few needles of dried rosemary chopped

1...Pre-heat the oven to 230c/450f/gas8
2...In a roasting tray, sear and colour the chopped bones in hot olive oil for about 6-8 minutes. Add the chopped onion, garlic, rosemary and thyme, and roast in the oven for another 20 minutes.
3...Place the bones and vegetables in a casserole and reserve. Add the white wine to the tray and boil to reduce by two-thirds. Add the tomato puree and water. Scrape the bottom of the tray to remove any caramelized bits, and pour this liquid into the casserole with the reserved bones. Bring to the boil, skim, and simmer for about 15 minutes. Strain through a fine sieve and reduce at full boil until you obtain about 150ml-5 fl oz. Taste, season with salt and pepper and reserve.

4...Preparing the lamb coating. Mix all the ingredients together thoroughly. Season with salt and pepper. Turn the temperature of the oven down to 220c/425f/gas7.

5...Cook the lamb. Heat the oil in a saute pan on top of the stove, and sear the meat on the meat side for 1 min until lightly coloured, then sear on the fat side for another 3 minutes. Lift the lamb onto the four reserved lamb bones and roast in the pre-heated oven for about 10 minutes. Remove and season with salt and pepper. Spread the mustard all over the meat (not on the bones), then press the meat only with the breadcrumb mixture, so it is completely covered. Roast again in the oven for another 12-15 minutes. Remove the lamb, reserve and rest on a warm plate, loosely covered with foil, for 2-3 minutes.

6...To serve: Place the lamb on a chopping board or dish and carve in front of your guests. Garnish as you please (see Chef's note) and serve the juice separately.

Chef's Note;- Ask your butcher to give you lamb that has been well hung for at least 10 days for best flavour and maximum tenderness.
A beautiful bouquet of watercress could be nicely arranged on a tray and a Provencal themes followed for vegetables, with such as Pommes Boulangeres, Ratatouille or French beans. Recipes are available in Raymond's book.

Recipe from 'Cooking For Friends' published by Hodder Headline

LE MANOIR AUX QUAT SAISONS
Great Milton, Oxford OX44 7PD. Tel: 01844 278881 Fax: 01844 278847
Proprietor/Chef:Raymond Blanc
Head Chef: Clive Fretwell
Open: All year. Hotel and Restaurant
Booking essential. Credit cards accepted. Wheelchair access.
Children of all ages welcome. Outside seating in the Summer. Log fires in winter. Seafood, game and vegetarian dishes created by Raymond Blanc and team. 2 Michelin stars. Relais & Chateau gold and red shields. AA 5 crowns and 4 Red stars. Egon Ronay 3 Stars and 85%.

Blanket of Pork with Capers and Paprika

1lb.8oz-700gm of pork shoulder, diced
2 small onions, finely sliced
1pt-570ml chicken stock
bouquet garni
2½oz-60gm butter
2oz-50gm flour
¼pt-150ml single cream
2 egg yolks
2 tbls paprika
1 tbls capers
1 red capsicum thinly sliced
1 tbls lemon juice
oil for frying
small amount of seasoned flour.

1...Toss the pork in the seasoned flour. Shake off the excess. Heat some oil in a frying pan and when hot lightly brown the pork pieces. Put to one side.
2...Melt the butter in a saucepan. Add the flour and paprika. Cook for a few minutes. Then pour in the chicken stock, stirring all the time until a sauce forms. Add the pork, bouquet garni, red capsicum and capers and simmer gently for about 1 hour. Or casserole in the oven. (Don't over cook or the meat will lose all of its flavour into the sauce).
3... When the pork is tender, add the cream. Heat through then add the egg yolks and lemon juice. Heat thoroughly but do not boil or the egg yolks will curdle.
4...Serve with basmati rice or new potatoes or even with a crust of puff pastry.

Oxford Blue Pork

Oxford Blue is a new cheese. Only three years old, and made specially for the Oxford Cheese Company by a small local cheese maker. It is a strong tasting cheese, salty like Danish blue but fuller flavoured like a Stilton. Currently only available at the Oxford Cheese Company.

1lb-450gm pork fillet, or 2 fillets of pork if they are sold like that
3oz-75gm Oxford Blue cheese, grated
8fl oz double cream, possibly less depending on taste
½pt-275ml good flavoured sock
2 tbls dry sherry or cider brandy
2 cox's apples, peeled, cored and thickly sliced
pepper, no salt
oil

1...Cut the pork fillet into 1"-2.5cm thick medallions. Heat some oil in a frying pan and brown the pork medallions on both sides. Push to the side of the pan.
2...Add the apple slices and quickly cook until a pale brown. About 2 minutes.
3...Raise the heat to its highest and add the stock and sherry or brandy. Push the pork back into the centre of the pan so that it can continue cooking in the pan juices. Reduce the juice by half.
4...Lower the heat and add the grated cheese. Cook until it melts into the reduced stock. Add the cream. You might not need to use all of it. Adjust the seasoning with the pepper. Salt shouldn't be needed as the cheese contains quite a lot.
Serve with saute potatoes and green beans.

Recipe from...

OXFORD CHEESE COMPANY
17 The Covered Market.   Tel:01865 721420
Proprietor: Robert Pouget and helped by son Sascha
Open: Mon - Fri 9am-5pm and Saturday 8.30-5pm.
Provides a wide range of French and British cheeses in excellent condition. As well as Oxford Blue look out for Gander goats cheese made at Goosey in Farringdon and North Cerney Goats cheese made in Gloucester.

Jambonnette of Free Range Chicken
served with
Mushroom and Goats Cheese Risotto

2 free range chicken legs
1 shallot
2 tbls of fresh fines herbs
salt and pepper
nutmeg
risotto:
4oz-110gm arborio rice; also wonderful made with pearl barley
1 shallot
1 clove garlic
2oz-50gm butter
5 morels, 5 ceps, 5 trompette mushrooms
2 tbls double cream
2oz-50gm goats cheese

1...Take the chicken legs and gently push back the skin to the end of the drum stick (keep the skin attached to the bone). Chop through the bone of the chicken 2cm's away from the end of the drum stick that is holding the skin to the bone. Remove the flesh from the bone and chop finely with the fines herbs, shallot and seasoning. Very gently push the flesh back into the skin. Don't press too hard!
2...Wrap the legs individually in cling film and then in tin foil. Poach for 20 minutes.
3...Risotto: Put the rice with the chopped shallot and garlic into a hot pan with the melted butter. Add the wild mushrooms and a small quantity of chicken stock. (If you are using dried mushrooms, soak them in hot water for 2 hours and use the mushroom flavoured water as stock). Continue simmering the rice and adding hot stock until the risotto rice is cooked. Grate the goats cheese and stir into the risotto with the cream. Mould the hot risotto into buttered timbales and turn out on to hot plates. Serve with the jambonnette and a sauce made from reduced chicken stock, marsala and cream. Serves 2 people.
From the kitchen of...

BATH PLACE HOTEL
4&5 Bath Place, Holywell Street, Oxford OX1 3SU.   Tel: 01865 791812 Fax: 01865 791835
Chefs: Jeremy Blake O'Conner and Eric Pages
Open: All year. Lunch 12noon-2pm (Sunday 12.30-2.30). Dinner 7pm-10pm (20.30 Fridays and Saturdays) 7pm-9.30 Sundays.
Non-smoking hotel and restaurant. Wide range of menus available. Full A la Carte, two and three course set lunch and five course Table D'Hote.
Vegetarians and special diets catered for.

Cask of a Thousand Years

Brewing beer has been going on in Oxford long before it became renowned as a place of learning. Virtually everyone from the small cottager to the keeper of the castle had their own home-brew. But then it was easy when they were living in the middle of malting barley country.

The first professional brewers in Oxford date from the thirteenth century. In the late fourteenth century 32 brewers were recorded paying the Poll Tax. Surprisingly, regulations were pretty stringent as price, quality and contamination were tested, and stiff penalties were paid if rules were breached.

As well as the professional brewers there was a good deal of home brewing going on amongst the colleges. Many had their own brewing houses. Queen's college brewed its own beer for 600 years until 1939. The building, in Fellows garden, still exists. Some of the best beer of this long era was said to be 'Trinity College' which supposedly turned out the fewest drunkards. It appears that in those day the beer with the lowest alcohol content was judged to be the best beer.

Brew Masters became extremely wealthy and figures of high standing and respectability, offering much employment for the towns people and revenue to the local tax offices. Many brewers stood for the important position of Town Mayor and between 1350 and 1500 ten brewers succeeded.

By the eighteenth century the prosperity of some brewers gave them opportunity to expand. In 1979 the William Hall Brewery bought out the old and established Swan's Nest Brewery. Then they went into partnership with the Tawney family and in 1896 became known as Hall's Oxford Brewery ltd. After that Hall's took over St Clements Brewery, Eagle Steam Brewery and Hanley's City breweries. It was a lucrative business and at one time employed as many as 60 horse drawn drays to deliver beer locally. A good deal of their beer was transported to other parts of the country either by water or rail. In 1926 Hall's were taken over by Allsop's and they were in turn taken over by Ind Coope. Hall's brewery building is now the Oxford Museum of Modern Art.

Another family of brewers that had a professional relationship with both the Hall's and Tawney families have managed to maintain their own personal identity. They have been brewing beer since 1782 in St Thomas Street near the city centre. This very same family is still brewing there today. They are the oldest family run business in the area and own over 135 public houses. Proud of their heritage they provide tours around their brewery and unlock a few secrets. You will taste the malt and smell the hops and yeast. Their College brew (7.4%) is their most exclusive cask beer and is only brewed in November. It is a traditional winter warmer with a smooth palate and wonderful afterglow.

Lemon Tree Rabbit Casserole

2 fresh skinned and cleaned rabbits
1 onion
2 carrots
2 sticks celery
1 leek
3 cloves garlic
fresh thyme, parsley, rosemary and tarragon
white peppercorns
bay leaf
1pt-570ml chicken stock
plain flour
1 dssrt spn dijon mustard
¼pt-150ml dry white wine
8oz-225gm button or flat mushrooms
olive oil for frying
2 tbls double cream

1...Cut the rabbit into 4-6 pieces depending on size. (Your butcher will do this for you). Fry gently in a cast iron pot.
2...Roughly chop the vegetables and garlic and add to the rabbit.
3...Strip the tarragon leaves from the stalks and put to one side. Add the tarragon stalks, parsley stalks, thyme, rosemary, bay leaf and peppercorns to the rabbit and vegetables. Keep frying, browning gently. Don't worry if the bottom of the pot becomes brown and appears a little burned. This is actually meat and vegetable residue, and as long as it isn't allowed to darken too much, will add flavour and colour to the finished sauce.
4...Remove from the heat and with a wooden spoon stir in 1 tbls plain flour, mixing well until a roux is formed around the meat and vegetables.
5...Return to a low heat and gently stir in the wine and half the chicken stock. Bring to the boil stirring continuously and add the remaining chicken stock.

6... Stir in the mustard, bring back to the boil, cover and place in a moderate oven for 1hr-1hr 15 minutes or until the meat is cooked through.
7...Lift the rabbit out of the pan with a slotted spoon and place in a deep serving dish.
8...In a separate saucepan gently fry the mushrooms until brown. Strain the rabbit sauce though a fine sieve onto the mushrooms. Add the cream and shredded tarragon leaves and simmer for 5 minutes. Adjust the seasoning and pour over the rabbit. Serve with mashed potato or celeriac and braised savoy cabbage.

Recommended wine: Cheras Futs de Chene, Domaine Sante 1994
        or
        Jackson Estate Marlborough Dry Riesling, N Z 1994

From the menu of...

THE LEMON TREE
Restaurant and Bar
268 Woodstock Rd, Oxford.   Tel: 018653 311936 Fax: 310021
Proprietor: Clinton Pugh
Chef: Guy Simpson
Open: All year. Noon-11pm. Brunch Sat and Sun 10am-1pm
Booking advised but casual callers welcome. Children welcome. Credit cards accepted. Wheelchair access.
Spacious restaurant with separate bar area, lounges. Ample parking. Outside seating.
Seafood, game and vegetarian dishes. International menu. All meats are free range and naturally reared.

Saute of Guinea Fowl

A wonderfully simple dish which is exquisite and brings out the true guinea fowl flavour.

1 plump guinea fowl
3oz-75gm shallots, finely chopped
6 fl oz-175ml dry white wine
6 fl oz-175ml double Jersey cream
1oz-25gm seasoned flour
2oz-50gm butter
salt and pepper

1...Cut the guinea fowl into 8 pieces (each breast in half and each leg in half, bones still intact).
2...Sweat the chopped shallots in half the butter. Add the remaining butter to the pan and saute the pieces of guinea fowl until lightly brown on all sides. Add seasoned flour.
3...Add the white wine, cream and seasoning. Stir. Cover. And leave on a gentle heat until tender. Approx 40 minutes.
4...Such a simple but fresh and natural tasting dish benefits from being served with fairly plain cooked vegetables such as steamed carrots, mangetout, broccoli or French beans.

From the kitchen of...

SHAVEN CROWN HOTEL
High Street, Shipton-under-Wychwood, Oxon OX7 6BA.   Tel/Fax:01993 830330
Proprietors: Brookes Family
Chef: Stanley Ryder
Open: All year.
Booking advised but casual callers welcome. Children welcome. Credit cards accepted.
Log fire in the Winter and outside seating in the Summer.
Seafood, game and vegetarian dishes.

The Covered Market

Oxford has two gourmet claims to fame. One is its prestigious Manoir aux Quat Saisons one of the finest restaurants in the country, made so by the exuberant Raymond Blanc. The other is its covered market.

The best time to visit the market is during the Christmas festive season, when a world reminiscent of Edwardian England, where hides of venison, unskinned hares and rabbits, birds still in feather hang from meat hooks out side stalls. Vegetarians may be offended by the sight, but if they want the best cheese or fresh pasta this is the place to come. Here is a place where food nostalgia, can be experienced to the full. That isn't to say it isn't worth a visit at any other time of year for it certainly is.

The site of todays covered market was taken in 1774. The area of Carfax in the centre of Oxford was always an open market, and had been since Mediaeval times. However as the city became busier the untidy scatter of market stalls got in the way of general traffic. A remedy was decided upon by the city and University. The stalls were to be rehoused in a specifically designed market building behind the High street. So, in 1774, meat, fish and vegetables under the supervision of a beadle (an officer of a church or college) were moved. During the Victorian era of the 1890's the market was rebuilt and covered and has since enjoyed a fluctuating prosperity often dependant on student population which has also fluctuated over the years.

Although most of the stall holders are purveyors of meat, fish, cheese, fruit and vegetables and unusual and exotic groceries, they too have been affected by the success of supermarkets. It has been found necessary to allow other types of trades enter the market to keep it alive. Such shops, have merged successfully and offer a wider interest to the visitor.

You're intention when visiting the covered market may only be to look but the produce is so irresistible there is no way you will be able to leave empty handed.

Simple Classic Salad Sauces

Mayonnaise

For the best results make by hand, which can be very therapeutic for impatient people.

1 egg yolk
1 small clove garlic
salt and pepper
2-3 tbls fresh lemon juice
½pt-275ml salad oil
2 tbls cold pressed extra virgin olive oil

1...Put the egg yolk, garlic, seasoning and lemon juice in a largish bowl. Beat together with a wooden spoon until pale.
2...Add 2 tspns of salad oil and beat with the wooden spoon. Repeat this until half the oil is mixed into the eggs.
3...Add 1 tbls of oil and beat until well amalgamated. Repeat until all the salad oil is used up.
4...Add the extra virgin olive oil. Beat well. If while adding the oil the sauce becomes too thick slacken off with a small drop of lemon juice. Store in a sealed container in the fridge until ready to use.

Marie Rose Sauce (luxury version)

4 tbls mayonnaise
1 tbls tomato ketchup, 1 tspn tomato puree
dash tabasco sauce, dash Worcester sauce
1 tspn made mustard
1 tbls double cream
dash lemon juice

1..Beat all theses ingredients together. Serve with cold fish a shell fish such as prawns, crab and salmon

Blue Cheese Sauce

4 tbls mayonnaise
4 tbls single cream
4oz-110gm sharp blue cheese such as Danish blue, grated
pepper, no salt

1...Place the ingredients in a blender and blend until smooth. Serve with all kinds of meat and salad leaves.

Puddings and Desserts

Tastes in puddings vary considerably. Some prefer something cool and refreshing or juicy and fruity and others prefer to indulge in something rich and gooey or creamy and moussy.

Choice of dessert is best dependent on what has gone before. Serve something light if the main meal has been rich and vice-versa. Avoid serving pastry or cream if either of these two ingredients have been involved in the starter or main dish. And again, avoid a fruit pudding if fruit has been involved in an earlier dish. These simple rules will ensure a balanced and interesting meal.

Lemon and Lime Sorbet

A simple dish, sharp and refreshing, to serve either between courses or as a tangy dessert after a rich dinner.

2 lemons
2 plump limes
8oz-225gm granulated sugar
½pt-275ml water
2 egg whites

1...Finely grate the zest from the lemons and limes. And squeeze the juice.
2...Put the sugar and water in a saucepan with the zest of the fruits. Heat gently until the sugar dissolves then boil rapidly for 5 minutes. Reduce the heat and simmer gently for 15 minutes.
3...Add the fruit juice to the syrup and then cool. Put in the freezer and freeze until almost but not quite solid.
4...Working very quickly, turn the frozen fruit juice into the bowl of an electric mixer. Add the egg white and whisk until the sorbet has fluffed up.
5...Tip back into a plastic container, cover and return to the freezer. To speed up freezing turn the freezer to super freeze for 40 minutes.

Oxford and Cambridge Pudding

The origins of this recipe seem to stem from the mid ninteenth century when, in Oxfordshire at least, a good many apricot trees were planted. They were provided by one of the Cartwright landlords; and at Blenheim Palace apricot trees were planted in the kitchen garden for the Marlboroughs. It is from here that California bought a variety of apricot from a Mrs Shipley which was deemed suitable for canning. The fruit stock is sill used to this day.

This is a rather special recipe created one would be led to believe in reverence of such a delicious fruit.

6oz-175gm shortcrust pastry
1lb-450gm fresh apricots
granulated sugar
3 standard eggs, separated
6 tbls double cream
3oz-75gm castor sugar

1...Roll out the pastry and line an 8"-20.5cm flan ring. Bake blind for 15 minutes. (you could use a ready baked flan case).
2...Halve the apricots and remove the stones. Stew very slowly in a saucepan in their own juice or on low in the microwave oven until soft. Sieve and sweeten to taste. Cool.
3...Beat the egg yolks into the cream and then beat into the apricot puree. Pour the mixture into the flan case and bake 190c/735f/gas5 for about 25 minutes or until the apricot custard is firm to the touch. Lower the temperature of the oven to 150c/300f/gas 2.
4...Whisk the egg white until stiff and add the 3oz-75gm castor sugar. Pile on top of the tart and return to the cool oven. Bake for 20 to 30 minutes. Serve warm or cold with whipped cream.

Self Pick Farms

What a wonderful concept the self-pick farm was. In its early days there was a clamour of excited voices praising the farms who opened their gates to the general public so that they could search among the brown earth rows for a choice cabbage, the best beans, the finest fruits... Customers could experience the thrill of picking something straight from the ground without having to grow it first. But the greatest advantage of all was the value, everything was cheaper, not only cheaper than the shops but cheaper than growing it yourself.

The emphasis on the self-pick expedition has changed slightly and is now more often than not considered part of a family day out. There are few simple, inexpensive pleasures left, yet to be out in the warm English sun harvesting a punnet of ripe juicy strawberries or perhaps ruby red raspberries, maybe both, knowing that you will soon be consuming them with some real dairy ice cream or perhaps a spoonful of thick, buttery, clotted cream.

If you are picking quantities to make jam, why not take the whole family and have a competition, who can pick the most in the shortest time, or who picks the best looking punnet, the prize? the biggest dish of strawberries for tea.

In some instances the Farm Shop has become a by-product of the self-pick farm. Here you can buy for a small extra premium, the freshly gathered crops already picked for you.

Farm Shops have developed considerably over the years. A lot of fun can be gained by venturing down dusty farm tracks in search of these, often barn converted, shops. A chance to see the workings of the farmyard and often a delight for children if the is some livestock to see - and much more than vegetables can now be bought. Many farms have gone into producing their own ice-creams, yogurts, sausages, jams and much, much, more, from the produce and livestock on their farm.

There is a self-pick farm and farm shop at Peach Croft Farm, Radley, Abingdon.

Upside-down Pear and Brandy Tart

¼ pt-275ml inexpensive brandy
5 packham pears
4oz-110gm castor sugar
2oz-50gm butter
finely grated rind of half a lemon

3oz-75gm plain flour
3oz-75gm ground almonds
4oz-110gm butter
1 tbls icing sugar
pinch of salt
1 small beaten egg

1...Peel the pears. Cut into quarters and remove the core. Cover and put to one side.
2...In a shallow, metal, saute or frying pan (must have a metal handle) put the butter and sugar. Place over a gentle heat until the butter has melted and the sugar dissolved. Raise the heat and cook until the sugar and butter begins to turn golden. Now add the brandy and maybe a little lemon juice. The mixture will bubble up. Lower the heat slightly and simmer until the sauce reduces by half.
3...Add the pears and lemon rind and simmer for five minutes until the pears are coated and golden. Move the pears around the pan to form a pattern. Put to one side.
4...Mix the flour and ground almonds together and rub in the butter. When you have fine bread crumbs add the icing sugar.
5...Beat the egg and use to bind the mixture together. Rest the pastry for 20 minutes in the fridge.
6...Roll out the pastry to about an inch larger than the pan. Lay the pastry on top of the pears and tuck the edges in.
7...Bake in a pre-heated oven. 220c/425f/gas7 for 25-30 minutes. Remove from the oven and turn upside down immediately onto its serving plate. But do not remove the pan. Let stand in a warm place for twenty minutes. Serve warm with whipped cream that has been dredged with molasses sugar.
Serves 4.

Deep Fried Elderflowers with a Summer Fruit Coulis, Wild Berries and Caramelized Nuts

This is a very unusual dish and is only available at Rosamund the Fair for 2-3 weeks in the year - when elderflowers are just out and the umbles are firm.

Batter
4oz-110gm plain flour
1oz-25gm castor sugar
1oz-25gm melted butter
2 eggs
½pt-275ml milk
4 firm elderflower heads, washed well
Wild berries
2oz-50gm each of blueberries, raspberries, red currants and blackcurrants
Summer fruit coulis
11oz-300gm mixed Summer fruits
4oz-110gm castor sugar
juice of ½ lemon
Caramelized nuts
2oz-50gm mixed nuts, almonds, pine kernels, pecan etc
2oz-50gm icing sugar
1 tbls Grand Marnier

1...First prepare the fruit coulis. Blend together in a processor the Summer fruits, castor sugar and juice of ½ lemon. Pass through a sieve to remove any small seeds. Chill until needed.
2...Next caramelize the nuts. Place the nuts, icing sugar and Grand Marnier in a small saucepan and stir over a gentle heat. When the contents start to caramelize stir the edges of the pan until the nuts crystalize. Remove from heat, turn the nuts out onto a cool surface and gently separate the nuts. Allow to cool and put to one side.
3...To make the batter; sieve the flour and salt in a bowl. Make a well in the centre and break in the eggs. Add the sugar and a small amount of milk and mix to a smooth batter. Beat in the rest of the milk and add the butter. Stand for 2-3 hours.

4...Wash the Summer fruits taking care not to bruise the flesh. Drain and chill until needed.
5...Heat oil in a deep fat fryer. Dip the elderflowers in the batter shaking off any excess batter and carefully place head first in hot oil until golden brown. Cut the stalk off the flower.
6...To serve. Arrange the cooked flowers on four pates. Scatter caramelized nuts and Summer fruits around the edge. Pour the coulis around the edge of the plate and serve immediately - while the flowers are still crisp.

From the menu of...

ROSAMUND THE FAIR
Cruising Restaurant
96 Godstow Road, Wolvercote, Oxford OX2 8PF.   Tel 01865 53370
Proprietor: Mr Mathews
Chefs: Tim Mathews and Sophia Goodford
Open: All year. Saturday and Sunday lunch 12.45. Wednesday - Sunday dinner. 7.45.
Booking is essential. Children welcome at lunch. Credit cards accepted.
Seafood and game dishes and vegetarian dishes on request.
A three hour cruise on the river Thames and through Oxford city centre. An experience not to be missed.

Red Berry Salad with Raspberry Sorbet and Strawberry Sauce

All the fruits for this recipe can be self picked or bought from Peach Croft Farm shop.
A light refreshing dessert ideal for any occasion and at any time of day.

1 small punnet each of: raspberries, strawberries, blackcurrants, red currants, blueberries, logan berries etc.
1-2 tbls icing sugar
Sorbet:
1 lb-450gm raspberries
8oz-225gm granulated sugar
1 egg white
Sauce:
8oz-225gm strawberries
4oz-110gm sugar
½ tbls lemon juice

1...First make the sorbet. Put ½pt-275ml water in a saucepan with the sugar. Heat slowly until the sugar has dissolved. Then bring to the boil and boil rapidly for 5 minutes. Add the raspberries and boil for 1 min.
2...Put the raspberries and the syrup in a blender and whiz to a puree. Pass through a sieve to remove the pips. Cool.
3...When cold pour the mixture into a plastic container that will go in the freezer and freeze for about 2 hours, or until almost frozen but not quite.
4...Turn the almost frozen sorbet into an electric mixing bowl. Add the egg white and beat until the mixture has ballooned out. Work very quickly so that the sorbet doesn't have time to melt. Turn back into the plastic container and freeze over night.
5...To make the sauce. Place the sugar in a saucepan with 6fl oz-175ml water. Heat gently until the sugar has dissolved then boil for 5 minutes. Add the hulled strawberries while the liquid is boiling then take off the heat. Stir in the lemon juice. Blend the strawberries and pass through a fine sieve to remove the pips (optional). Cool and store in the fridge. It is best to use this sauce the same day as it is made. After that it begins to loose its bright taste.

6...Wash the fruits gently, but only if absolutely necessary. Pat dry with kitchen paper. Tip the fruits into a roomy bowl so that they don't squash down too much. Sprinkle over the icing sugar and leave to stand in a cool place for 1 hr. Serve in glass Sunday dishes with generous scoops of the sorbet and some of the sauce or arrange artistically on large plates. Looks good served in soup plates.
Serves 4-6 people.

Recipe using ingredients from...

PEACH CROFT FARM SHOP
Pick Your Own
Peach Croft Farm, Radley, Oxon.   Tel 01235 520094 Fax 522688
Proprietors: W.J and J Homewood
Chef: L Thomas
Open; Winter 9am-5pm and Summer 9am-7pm. Christmas 9am-6pm
Casual callers and children welcome. Credit cards accepted. Wheelchair access.
Outside seating. Vegetarian Dishes.
PYO Asparagus, strawberries and raspberries in season.

Dexters' Poached Pear Tart with Caramel Sauce and Vanilla Ice Cream

Jamie Dexter-Harrison is renowned for his poached pear tart and is one of the restaurants most requested desserts.

4 medium sized firm pears
8oz-225gm castor sugar
1 vanilla pod, split. ½ lemon
12oz-350gm puff pastry, thawed if frozen
Caramel sauce:
12oz-350gm castor sugar
½pt-275ml whipping cream
cold water
To serve:
4 scoops of vanilla or ginger ice cream
icing sugar to dust

1...Peel and core the pears and place in a medium sized saucepan with the split vanilla pod, castor sugar and lemon with just enough water to cover the pears. Cover the saucepan. Bring the water to the boil, then reduce the heat and poach the pears until they are soft. Remove the pears from the heat and leave them in the cooking liquor.
3...To make the sauce, place the castor sugar in a small saucepan and pour cold water over to just cover the sugar. Simmer over a low heat, do not stir, until the sugar caramelizes. Remove from the heat and, using a wooden spoon, immediately stir in the whipping cream. Stir vigorously until smooth then transfer into a pouring jug.
5...Roll out the puff pastry to 1/8"-2mm thick. Place it in the fridge for 10 minutes to allow it to rest. Remove from the fridge and cut 4x 5"-12.7cm circles.
6...Place the circles of pastry on a baking sheet and put a pear in the centre of each. Place in a pre-heated oven 220c/425f/gas7 for 9 minutes.
7...To serve. Place the pear tarts on large plates. Warm the caramel sauce and pour the sauce over and around the tarts. Dust with icing sugar and serve 1 scoop of ice cream with each tart.

From the menu of...

DEXTERS' RESTAURANT
Market Place, Deddington, Oxon OX15 0SE.   Tel:01869 338813
Chef/Proprietor: Jamie Dexter-Harrison. AA 2 Rosettes
Open: All year. Tuesday-Saturday. Lunch 12 noon-2pm and Dinner 7pm-11pm
Booking advised but casual callers welcome. Credit cards accepted.
Game and vegetarian dishes. Fresh fish dishes a speciality.

Ginger Fruit Compote

1lb-450gm dried fruit (apricots, prunes, figs, pears, peaches, dates)
4-8 pieces of stem ginger in syrup depending on how much you like ginger.
1 large cinnamon stick
8 green cardamom pods
1 pt-570ml fresh orange juice

1...Soak the fruit in the orange juice until plump (overnight).
2...Put in an enamel or stainless steel saucepan and simmer the fruit and orange juice with the spices until the fruit is as soft as you like it. You may have to top up with water if the juice evaporates too quickly.
3...Allow to cool. Remove the cinnamon stick and cardamom pods. Chop the ginger as fine or coarse as you like it and add to the compote.
4...Serve warm with custard, whole milk yogurt, cream or ice cream. Alternatively: layer the compote in glass dishes with amaretti biscuits and creamy yogurt or fromage frais.

Recipe supplied by...

FRUGAL FOOD
Wholefood Grocer
17 West Saint Helen Street, Abingdon, Oxon OX14 5BL   Tel: 01235 522239
Proprietor: Val Stoner
Open: All year. 9ish-5.30 (5pm Saturday) Closed 24th Dec-4th Jan.
Mail order service for light weight items i.e. Herbs and spices.
Real Cheese. Organic wine. Handmade Chocolates.

Afternoon Tea

Afternoon tea or coffee and cakes are abundant in and around Oxford. From three thirty onwards tearooms and cafes are filled with the mellifluous sound of teaspoons tinkling against the side of tea cups; and the gentle consumption of home-made cakes, freshly baked scones and little dishes of cream, heralds a satisfying end to a fun filled day.

Banbury Cakes

The original recipe for Banbury cakes was somewhat different to that of today. First recorded in the late sixteenth century, it was a spicy fruit cake risen with dough and before cooking wrapped in some plain bread dough. Today the recipe calls for flaky pastry and the filling is a rich mixture of fruits, spices and rum, more like a mincemeat mixture than a yeast cake. They are similar to Eccles cakes the main difference being the oval shape unlike the round Eccles cake.

The Original Cake Shop run by the brown family until it closed in 1967 was said to make the best Banbury cakes ever and is still talked about by those who can remember. A history of the Banbury cake can be viewed at the Banbury museum. The cakes are readily available in many cake shops in the area.

12oz-350gm flaky pastry
8oz-225gm mixed peel, finely chopped
8oz-225gm currants
4oz-110gm butter
½ tspn each of ground allspice and nutmeg
¼ tspn ground cinnamon
1 tbls dark rum
egg white for brushing
granulated sugar for sprinkling

1...Pre-heat the oven to 220c/425f/gas7.
2...Cream the butter and mix in the peel, currants, spices and rum. Put to one side in a cool place.
3...Roll out the flaky pastry to ¼"-0.5cm thick. Cut into rounds with a 3"-8cm cutter.
4...Put 1 hpd tspn of the filling in the centre of each round. Moisten the edges and pinch them together to make the cakes flatish and oval.
5...Grease a baking sheet and place on the cakes with the joins underneath. With a sharp knife cut make three slits across the centre. Brush with egg white and sprinkle generously with the granulated sugar. Bake for 20-25 minutes. They should not be too dark.
Banbury cakes are best eaten warm so that they melt in the mouth.

Let's Bake a Cake

It is a great sadness that the weekly tradition of baking a cake has drifted away. Yet the large display of cakes on supermarket shelves and the number of cake shops and patisseries around, and, the number of people who frequent local tea-rooms for a cup of tea and a piece of cake, suggests the tradition of eating cake is very much with us.

Lack of time, for so many women, the usual baker of cakes, is probably the main reason for the demise of the home-baked cake.

Cake is often viewed as something special, a marker for a that personal event like a birthday, a wedding, a christening, a retirement or an anniversary. Also, universally it is made to represent religious festivals such as Christmas and Easter.

Cake making isn't at all difficult, in fact it is difficult to go wrong, provided you follow the instructions to the letter. The most important rule is, always measure your ingredients. Unless you make cakes on a regular basis, (and even then lack of concentration can result in a flop) don't be tempted to guess the measurements. The smallest discrepancy can give imperfect results. Secondly, cake mixtures should be treated with respect. The aim is to get as much air into the mixture as possible, then keep it there. In other words once the beating, whisking or creaming is complete the dry ingredients should be carefully folded in.

Here are a few extra tips. 1. Use soft margarine or make sure the butter is *very* soft. 2. Have the ingredients at room temperature not straight out of the fridge. 3. Use self raising flour. 4. Size 2 eggs are best. 5. Don't bake in too hot an oven.

Cake Making Methods.

Rubbing In: Normally used for fruit cakes. The flour and butter is rubbed together into fine breadcrumbs, the fruit, eggs etc are then added.

Whisking: Swiss roll and gateau sponges. Usually fatless. The eggs and sugar are whisked over the saucepan of hot water until trebled in volume. The flour is very carefully folded in.

Creaming: Victoria Sponge, and the most popular method of cake making. Fat and sugar is beaten together until light and fluffy. Then the eggs are gradually beaten in. The flour is carefully folded in at the end.

Melting: Gingerbread. Butter, sugar, syrup and liquid are melted together with the fruit, cooled slightly, then the flour is stirred in to make a batter.

Mincemeat and Nut Tart

3.½oz-100gm butter melted
8oz-225gm digestive biscuits crushed
4oz-110gm walnut pieces roughly chopped
1lb-450gm good quality mince meat
2oz-50gm raisins
1oz-25gm arrowroot
3fl oz-75ml orange juice

10"-26cm loose bottomed flan ring

1...Mix together the melted butter and crushed biscuit and press into the bottom and sides of the lightly greased flan ring.
2...Set the oven to 190c/350f/gas5.
3...In a saucepan gently simmer together the walnuts, mincemeat, raisins in 3/4pt-400ml water for about 10 minutes. (Not too long)
4...Dissolve the arrowroot in the orange juice and add to the fruit and nut mixture. Return to the heat and simmer until the mixture thickens. Do not boil or the mixture will turn thin again. Turn the mixture into the biscuit base and bake for 10 minutes.
Cool thoroughly. Remove the loose flan ring and serve with whipped cream

N.B. Brandy or whisky can be used instead of orange juice.

Chocolate and Chestnut Roulade

4 large eggs
4oz-110gm castor sugar
3oz-75gm self-raising flour
1oz-25gm cocoa powder
<u>*filling*</u>
½pt-275ml double cream
1 or 2 tbls brandy
1 small tin sweet chestnut puree

1...Line and grease a swiss roll tin approx 12"x9"-30.5x23cm and pre-heat oven to 190c/375f/gas5.
2...Break the eggs into a mixing bowl. Add the sugar and whisk until light and foamy. This will take about 8-10 minutes using an electric whisk.
3...When the egg and sugar mixture is pale and creamy very carefully fold the sifted flour and cocoa. It is essential that you maintain the bulkiness of the mixture.
4...Pour into the swiss roll tin and lightly level the surface. Bake in the pre-heated oven for 15-20 minutes or until the centre is firm and springy.
5...Lay a piece of greaseproof paper on the work surface and sprinkle with castor sugar. Loosen the edges of the sponge and turn out onto the greaseproof paper. With a sharp knife cut off the outside edges off the sponge, then while still hot roll the sponge up.
6...Filling: mix together the chestnut puree and brandy. Whip the double cream and fold into the chestnut mixture. When the sponge is cold, unroll, spread over the chestnut cream and re-roll.
7...Dredge generously with icing sugar. Keep in the fridge until ready to serve.

This is also delicious served as a dessert with chocolate sauce.

Carrot Cake

A very good carrot cake can be had at the Nosebag.

12 fl oz sunflower oil
12oz-350gm demerara sugar
6 size 3 eggs, beaten
1 tspn vanilla essence
6oz-175gm walnuts, chopped small
1lb-450gm carrots, finely grated
2oz-50gm desiccated coconut
2 tspn bi-carb
2 tspns baking powder
2 tspns ground ginger
1 tspn salt
12oz-350gm plain flour
Filling and Topping
8oz-225gm cream cheese
4oz-110gm butter
6oz-175gm icing sugar
chopped walnuts

1..Pre-heat the oven to 180c/350f/gas4. Grease a 9"-23cm cake tin and dust with flour.
2...Beat together the oil, sugar, eggs and vanilla essence until light and foamy.
3...Sift together the flour, bi-carb and baking powder. Stir into the mixture along with the rest of the ingredients.
4...Pour the mixture, which will be quite runny into the prepared cake tin and bake in the oven for 1 to 1½hours. Test with a skewer in the centre of the cake which will come out clean if cooked. Cool in the tin for a few minutes then turn onto a wire rack and cool completely.
5...Beat together all the filling ingredients with the exception of the walnuts.
6...Split the cake in half. Spread half the mixture over the bottom half. Put back the top half and spread over the rest of the mixture. Sprinkle with the chopped walnuts. This is quite a large cake and will serve several people.

Chocolate and Ginger Crunch

1 lb-450gm of the best dark chocolate you can afford
small packet ginger biscuits, roughly crushed
4oz-110gm crystalised ginger, chopped
2 tbls golden syrup
finely grated zest of and orange
juice of an orange
4oz-110gm butter
4oz-110gm chopped mixed nuts or desiccated coconut

1...Line a swiss roll tin with greaseproof paper.
2...Break up the chocolate and melt in either in a saucepan or in the microwave with the golden syrup and orange zest. Dice the butter and stir it into the melted chocolate with the orange juice.
3   Stir in the dry ingredients. Pour into the swiss roll tin and press down. When set, cut into squares of fingers.

Pithivier

Undoubtedly Raymond Blanc has had an influence on Oxford. And when you look at restaurant menus you can't help but notice an element of friendly rivalry. It is nice to know that a good meal can be had in many local establishments even if not set in the special and luxurious surroundings of Le Manoir and not cooked by the great man himself.
This recipe has been included as a celebration of the French influence that has come to Oxford over the last fifteen years.

1lb-450gm puff pastry
4oz-110gm icing sugar
4oz-110gm softened butter
4oz-110gm ground almonds
4 size 3 eggs
2 tspns almond essence
2 tbls apricot puree

1...Cream together the butter and icing sugar. Mix in the ground almonds. Beat the eggs and add to the mixture. Add the almond essence.
2...Divide the pastry in half and roll out two circle 8"-20.5cm in diameter. Make one circle a fraction larger then the other.
3...Place the smaller circle on a baking sheet. Spread over the apricot puree. Then spread on top of this the almond cream to 3/4"-1.5cm from the edge.
4...Moisten the edges and lay the second circle of pastry on top. Press the edges well together, then knock up the edges with your finger tips. Liberally brush the surface with beaten egg. Score a pattern on the pastry with a knife or the prongs of a fork.
5...Place in the oven pre-heated to 200c/400f/gas6 for 20 minutes. Then lower the temperature and cook for a further 15 minutes. Serve warm with cool whipped cream.

Oxford Blue Scones

8oz-225gm self raising flour
1 tspn bi-carb
½ tspn salt
large pinch dry English mustard
1oz-25gm butter or margarine
4oz-110gm Oxford blue cheese, grated
¼pt-150ml creamy milk
1 small egg, beaten
milk and grated parmesan or ground paprika for glazing

1...Pre-heat oven 200c/400f/gas7
2...In a large mixing bowl sift together the flour, bi-carb, salt and dried mustard
3...Rub in the butter until the mixture resembles fine breadcrumbs.
4...Stir in the grated Oxford blue. Mix in the egg and enough milk to make a soft but not sticky dough.
5...Gather the mixture together and briefly and lightly knead into a ball. Flatten out this ball and place on an oiled baking sheet. Flatten out. Brush with milk and sprinkle over the parmesan or paprika. Score the dough into eight segments (not all the way through). Bake for 20-25 minutes or until golden.
6...Cool. Serve with rich country butter and perhaps some smoked salmon.

N.B. other strong cheeses can be used such as cheddar and stilton.

Towns and Villages

Abingdon. Situated on the Thames there is plenty of river activities. A typical town with an attractive market square overlooked by a grand town hall. Plenty of historical buildings to visit including the remains the abbey.
** Frugal Food ** Peach Croft Farm Shop ** The Cottage Bakery **

Banbury. Dating back to Saxon times this is now a busy albeit attractive industrial town with a busy shopping centre. Famous for the Banbury Cross which was replaced in 1859 after the original one was destroyed. A must is to eat its famous Banbury cakes at on of the towns tea shops.
** Banbury Cakes **

Burford. Another town of architectural and historical interest. Boasts the second largest church in Oxfordshire. Set in the Windrush valley, the town is delightful and although ancient truly established itself on the riches of the wool industry. Most buildings are of Cotswold stone. The high street slips steeply down to the Windrush river, where there is plenty of riverside leisure.
** Inn For All Seasons **

Deddington. Built on a hill, and in Saxon times it was called Daedintun. Gourmets will be pleased to know there is a good market place. The town has lots of historical character, soft toned buildings and traditional old Inns.
** Dexter's Restaurant **

Godstow/Wolvercote. A small village that's shown at its best if you take the three mile walk from Oxford along the river. You will pass over pretty bridges and a crystal, and will be able to refresh yourself at the famous Trout Inn. It was at the now ruined nunnery that Fair Rosamund, mistress of Henry II was educated.
** Rosamund the Fair **

Great Milton and Little Milton. A short drive out of Oxford and made famous by Raymond Blanc at the ** Manoir Aux Quat Saisons ** At Little Milton is the site of ** Halcyon Herbs **

Iffley. Another place that is best reached by foot or on water. Set out along the towpath and a short walk out of the city into the suburbs brings you to this delightful riverside place.

Oxford. The oldest English speaking university in the world. Set on the river Thames it is of great architectural interest. There is plenty of water activities for the leisure minded.
** Alternative Tuck Shop ** Cafe Moma ** St Aldates Coffee House ** Bunters Delicatessen ** Fasta Pasta ** Stroff's Speciality Sausages ** The Oxford Cheese Company ** Bath Place Hotel ** Cherwell Boat House ** Gee's ** Greek Taverna ** The Lemon Tree **

Shipton-under-Wychwood. Wychwood Forest sits above the river Evenlode and was once a large and great Royal hunting ground. Little of the forest is left today. Beneath the remains of this wood lies many picturesque villages. of which Shipton-under-Wychwood is one.
** Shaven Crown Hotel **

Witney. A typical Cotswold style market town just outside Oxford. As long ago as the thirteenth century it made the luxurious, woollen Witney blanket and eventually became famous for it all over the world. The town is surrounded with old Mills and millers cottages and Blanket Hall in the high street was built to weigh and measure the blankets.
** Bean Bag Wholefoods **

Woodstock. Blenheim Palace, the country's largest house and landscaped by the world famous landscape gardener 'Capability' Brown is the initial draw to Woodstock. But once there an extremely attractive town is to be found despite the intervention of modern buildings. There is plenty of choice for food lovers of restaurants, inns and tearooms.
** The Bear Hotel ** The Feathers Hotel ** La Galleria **

Index of Contributors

Cafes and Tearooms

28 Alternative Tuck Shop. Oxford. Tel: 792054
36 Cafe Moma. Oxford. Tel: 01865 722733
54 St Aldates Coffee House. Oxford. Tel: 01865 245952

Caterers

Entries are welcome for the next edition of this book

Public Houses

Entries are welcome for the next edition of this book

Note to Businesses
If you cook your own speciality dishes,
or if you run a speciality shop,
or sell or manufacture a local product or ingredient
and would like to be featured in the next edition
of this book, please contact
Travelling Gourmet Publications

Producers and Suppliers

31 Beanbag Wholefoods. Witney. Tel: 01993 773922
17 Bunters Delicatessen. Oxford.
34 Fasta Pasta. Oxford. Tel: 01865 241973
79 Frugal Food. Abingdon. Tel: 01235 522239
25 Halcyon Herbs. Little Milton. Tel: 01865 89180
76 Peach Croft Farm Shop. Radley. Abingdon. Tel: 01235 520094
43 Stroff's Speciality Sausages. Oxford. Tel: 01865 200922
19 The Cottage Bakery. Abingdon. Tel: 01235 520972
61 The Oxford Cheese Company. Oxford. Tel: 01865 721420

Restaurants/Bistros/Brasseries

62 Bath Place Hotel/Restaurant. Oxford. Tel: 01865 791812
22 Cherwell Boathouse. Oxford. Tel: 01865 52746
78 Dexter's Restaurant. Deddington. Tel: 01869 338813
46 Gee's. Oxford. Tel: 01865 53540
51 Greek Taverna. Summertown. Tel: 01865 511472
24 Inn For All Seasons. Burford. Tel: 01451 844324
16 La Galleria. Woodstock. Tel: 01993 813381
58 Le Manoir Aux Quat Saisons. Great Milton. Tel: 01844 278881
74 Rosamund the Fair. Wolvercote. Tel: 01865 53370
66 Shaven Crown Hotel. Shipton-under-Wychwood. Tel: 01993 830330
12 The Bear Hotel/Restaurant. Woodstock. Tel: 01993 811511
18 The Feathers Hotel/Restaurant. Woodstock. Tel: 01993 812291
64 The Lemon Tree. Oxford. Tel: 01865 311936

Conversion Tables

All these are *approximate* conversions which have either been rounded up or down. In a few recipes it has been necessary to modify them very slightly. Never mix metric and imperial measurements in one recipe; stick to one system or the other

WEIGHTS	
½ oz	10 g
1	25
1½	40
2	50
3	75
4	110
5	150
6	175
7	200
8	225
9	250
10	275
12	350
13	375
14	400
15	425
1 lb	450
1 ¼	550
1 ½	700
2	900
3	1.4kg
4	1.8
5	2.3

VOLUME	
1 fl oz	25 ml
2	50
3	75
5 (¼ pint)	150
10 (½)	275
15 (¾)	400
1 (pint)	570
1 ¼	700
1 ½	900
1 ¾	1 litre
2	1.1
2 ¼	1.3
2 ½	1.4
2 ¾	1.6
3	1.75
3 ¼	1.8
3 ½	2.0
3 ¾	2.1
4	2.3
5	2.8
6	3.4
7	4.0
8 (1 gal)	4.5

MEASUREMENTS	
¼ inch	0.5 cm
½	1.0
1	2.5
2	5.0
3	7.5
4	10.0
6	15.0
7	18.0
8	20.5
9	23.0
11	28.0
12	30.5

OVEN TEMPERATURE

Mark 1	275°F	140°C
2	300	150
3	325	170
4	350	180
5	375	190
6	400	200
7	425	220
8	450	230
9	475	240

Index of Recipes

Asparagus soup 15
Aubergine and basil mousse, hot, with pesto and spinach 12
Avocado Cardinale 16

Baked egg and smoked ham en cocotte 31
Banbury cakes 81
Beef and onion stew 51
Blanket of pork with capers and paprika 60
Brown trout, pan fried with parsley butter 49

Carpaccio of beef with mixed hot leaves 26
Carre d' Agneau Provencal 58
Carrot cake 85
Chicken and basil sausage 22
Chicken liver pate 19
Cod fillet with claytonia and tomato dressing 46
Cranberry and turkey sandwich, spiced 28
Chocolate and ginger crunch 86
Chocolate and chestnut roulade 84
Colcannon 55

Dexter's poached pear tart with caramel sauce and vanilla ice cream 78

Elderflowers, deep fried with summer fruit coulis, wild berries and caramelized nuts 74
Game pies, little 29
Ginger fruit compote 79
Guinea fowl, saute 66

Jambonnette of free range chicken 62

Lamb boulanger 54
Lemon Tree rabbit casserole 64
Lemon and lime sorbet 70

Mincemeat and nut tart 83
Mushroom and courgette loaf 36

Old Speckled hen beef 52
Oxford baked egg 37
Oxford Blue pork 61
Oxford Blue scones 88
Oxford brawn sauce 42

Oxford and Cambridge pudding 71

Pesto sauce 32
Pear tart, poached, Dexter's 78
Pear and brandy tart, up side down 73
Pizza tart 1990 33
Pithivier 87
Pork with capers and paprika 52
Primavera 34
Pumpkin and leek risotto 38

Quiche lorraine 39

Red berry salad with raspberry sorbet and strawberry sauce 76
Raspberry sorbet 76

Salmon, baked, with sorrel sauce 48

Sauces:
   blue cheese dressing 68
   brawn sauce, Oxford 42
   caramel sauce 78
   hazelnut oil and lemon dressing 43
   mayonnaise 68
   pesto sauce 32
   rose marie 68
   shallot and chilli dressing 18
   sorrel sauce 48
   strawberry sauce 76
   summer fruit coulis 74
   tomato dressing 46

Scallops Mousse, pan fried, with shallot and chilli dressing 18
Seafood boudin with mangetout and herb butter sauce 43
Sesame rabbit salad 41
Sicillian sausage with pasta 44
Stifatho 51

Tjatjiki 17

Vegetarian lasagne 40
Vegetarian sausage with hazelnut oil and lemon dressing 43
Vegetarian scotch eggs 31
Wiltshire ham and green peppercorn terrine 24

Angela Hewitt has been interested in food all her life. Her love of good food stems from her early childhood when she lived with her Aunt and Uncle. They used to run a home-cooked meat and pie shop. Her aunt was a brilliant cook of traditional British food and the table was always plied with good home baking, fresh vegetables, delicious roasts and tasty, natural flavoured stews, with not a stock cube or frozen pea in sight.

For eighteen years Angela was involved in the catering business before taking up food and travel writing.

She started off cooking in a small guest house before taking up the catering concessions at 2 Island yacht clubs.

She opened her own restaurant 'Lugleys' in Lugley Street on the Isle of Wight in 1980. Within a year her cooking was being recommended by Egon Ronay's good food guide. Soon she was in all of the guides and was awarded 2 rosettes by the AA Good Restaurant Guide.

After 14 yrs of anti-social and very tiring hours she decided on a career change in the hope of discovering a more relaxing life style. Since then she has written several regional cookery books, magazine articles and made radio and TV appearances.

Her main interest is in regional and British food and home cooking and how it is changing and affecting people with the influences of foreign imports. The best people to ask she realised, were those people doing it. The food producers, and cooks of each region. So the 'What's Cooking' series was born.

The books are not meant to be a critique but a celebration of food in all its guises. There is a place for everything, and although she is a firm believer of real cooking and the use of fresh and local produce she also knows caterers have to make a living and that the ideal is not always possible and indeed not a true reflection of what is happening on the local food scene.

Whether it is fast food or gourmet food there is a place for it all.

The 'What's Cooking' series is aiming to give a balanced look at food and sometimes to redress the balance when extremes arise.